Psychology of God and the Soul

Edward Conklin Ph.D.

Edward Conklin

ISBN 978-0-9906457-8-8

Edward Conklin

Dedication

I dedicate this work to the young, who not told, usually have to find out the hard way. Let each make the effort to comprehend both self and soul, and let each spend their allotted days filling a brief life with some happy moments.

Edward Conklin

Acknowledgments

I gratefully acknowledge and thank family, friends, and teachers for their love and encouragement. I am indebted to many who have come before and without whose tireless efforts, findings, and recorded words, this work would not have been written. I acknowledge and thank Ms. Natalie Harley for her editorial assistance and patience.

Edward Conklin

Published works by Edward Conklin Ph.D.

Psychology of God and the Soul. (2016). Amazon Kindle and CreateSpace.

Meditations on God and the Soul. (2015). Amazon Kindle and CreateSpace.

A Brief Guide to God and the Soul. (2015). Amazon Kindle and CreateSpace.

In the Beginning: A New Theory of the First Religion. (2014). Amazon Kindle and CreateSpace.

Cosmos, God, and Soul. (2014). Amazon Kindle and CreateSpace.

From Tool-maker to God Maker. (2014). Amazon Kindle and CreateSpace.

Waves Rough and Smooth & the Deep Blue Sea. (2014). Amazon Kindle and CreateSpace.

Getting Back Into the Garden of Eden. (1998). University Press of America.

Introduction

Beginning in childhood humans have an innate curiosity about what exists and where things come from. Growing up and maturing there is spontaneously sensed both individual limitation, and a vastness of space and time. Eventually personal space is limited to a geographical area and time is structured by relative watch and clock schedules. Busy with life, the vastness of reality usually recedes into the background. Yet, when time permits, humans tend to ponder about what exists. Individuals vaguely sense some kind of continuum from the physical to a metaphysical reality, and a yearning by some to casually or ardently explore it.

Unfortunately in Europe and Western countries, innate inquisitiveness about the metaphysical is channeled into the artificial and immature thinking of theistic religions. Many humans on earth hold the view of a human-like first father god. Sharing this subjective view through participation in rituals and holidays, is the shallow depth of metaphysics that an adult manages to acquire in life. The average person prefers ideas associated with a human-like god and pairs them with emotions of faith for their metaphysical reality.

Religious services are offered for one to two hours usually on the weekend. A theistic service consists of casual attention directed to belief and faith in a human-like first father god. The propensity to explore and learn about physical and metaphysical reality is effectively blocked by blind belief in a god who is said to know everything. Modern science has dramatically increased human knowledge of both physical and metaphysical realties. While it is realistic to look upward into infinite space in seeking the origin of existence, it is no longer feasible, reasonable, or sane to think of it to be a human-like first father god. Rather, the origin of existence is a cosmological force that moves all things into, through and out of relative existence.

An individual can learn about many things during the course of life. What is valuable is to spend a portion of daily living to investigate and to better comprehend life and death.

Where has life come from and how is it connected to the origin of the universe? Does a human-like god exist? Do humans have a soul that survives physical death? The following will explore the psychology of these metaphysical topics.

In philosophy an argument is defined as, an attempt to persuade or convince another to a point of view or course of action. My argument in this work is that all human-like gods are the adult version of a childhood imaginary companion, and are further elaborated on by human artistic imagination. I also argue that the human soul is a real triune force that forces life to live, and that it is a continuation of a sole cosmological force.

Beginning

A human-like god is a way of locating the beginning of the environment and life in space and time that extend seemingly without beginning or end. An arbitrarily inserted first father is a psychologically devised means of knowing a beginning.

For most westerners, it does not seem at all unusual to think there is a human-like male god, a parent figure that made all things. Yet, a human-like god is an outdated way of looking at the origin of existence. A human-like god is a human manufactured symbol for a natural (Latin natus, to be born) progression through a dimensional universe of space and time. A human-like god is superimposed over the mysterious motion of a cosmological multiverse.

A human-like god serves only as a shortcut pointer to designate a deeply felt, yet difficult to define connection with a real universal motion. Each person, whether knowingly or unknowing, is a mysterious and profound continuation of the undeniable immediate motion of the cosmos. Noticed or unnoticed, there ever exists a connection of the environment and life with a cosmological force, field, or ground. The bare superficial notion of a human-like god is the way humans call attention to and make known this profound fact.

Based on the observed effects of a moving cosmos, a cosmological force though not observed, can be inferred to exist. There exists a cosmological force that forces the cosmos to be in a relative motion of energy, and forms. Properly understood, this comprehension should be uplifting for humans; that each individual body and brain is a continuation of what moves the cosmos. No imaginary companion of an artistically crafted human-like god is needed to explain existence.

Life and the environment are often difficult to comprehend and to regulate. An individual meets with conflict from both inside and outside of the body. There exists genetic cellular and organ dysfunctions, accidents, illness, microorganisms, and conflict with fellow humans and the environment. Encountering harm, many humans turn to what first brought faulty life into existence; the conception of a human-like god.

For many who seek the origin of existence, attention is turned not to objective clues in the environment but to a subjectively conceived idea. Humans prefer to overlook and not see the internal function of life to be a continuation of the external immediate environment. Instead, some careless humans prefer to travel back in time to a past human-like parent.

Many humans can proceed through the hazards of living only by tracing their existence to a genealogical origin. Humans need a direction to go in life, and the direction should be a good one. For many, the good must be similar to what provides care for children and young adults.

To ascend to a higher or better level of human thinking and behaving, there must be a higher level. The higher and better level for most is what transcends what is here and now and this is a beginning that exists far beyond all things in space and time. The knowledge of this beginning is demarcated by insertion of a human-like god. The traditional way to human comprehension of the beginning of the environment and life is to imagine it to be a first father god.

To go in the direction of the known is preferred over the unknown, and therefore attention is directed to a familiar parent-like figure. Ironically, relief from a faulty life is sought by seeking the beginning of it. The function of life is not traced to the reality of the earth environment but to an imagined ancestor, an embellished human-like forefather god.

For theists, the beginning of life is not traced to sex and reproduction as argued by Sigmund Freud or to the observed environment as argued by Charles Darwin. Instead, theists turn to a beginning subjectively conceived, non-observable and non-biological human-like first father god. The notion of a human-like god is a delusion or mistaken idea and a type of attribution error.

Attribution Error

Life is an aesthetic experience of sensations and objects. It is certain that no human has ever had sensations of a beginning time of the universe, therefore humans have not ever perceived a time of origin. Humans have only a conception of a beginning. To make the beginning appear for early human comprehension, a non-phenomenal, not perceived from sensations beginning was conceived as human-like.

The Middle East derived Western human-like god is a human attribution error. The error is in attributing the origin of existence to be a genealogical first father god who approximately six thousand years ago, suddenly and inexplicably made all things. The event certainly begs a question; what was the god doing prior to the sudden event? The supposed timeless tribal ancestor god first appeared in time to make the environment and living forms, and eventually strolled in the garden in "…the cool of the day." (Genesis 3:8)

Of the many evolved living species, humans observed themselves to make many unique things, such as tools, weapons, and shelters. Since humans are the best makers something human-like had to make the environment and life. The simplistic and egocentric conception is that the beginning of existence is human-like. There is an over-weening pride in a human-like beginning, that a much greater human-like intelligence began the reality sequence of events. As the proverb says, "Pride goeth before destruction, and a haughty spirit before a fall." (Proverbs 16:18)

The ongoing daily fall of humans comes in part from overconfidence in being protected by an imaginary companion. Humans foolishly forge ahead to place themselves in harm's way to meet psychological injury and physical destruction over and over interminably. Whoever encourages love of a conceived humanlike beginning, suggests and instills a false confidence in diffident humans. A human-like model god is an instructive apish conception; a way of encouraging others to follow, as in monkey see, monkey do.

When it comes to comprehending human origin, some portion of the population long ago and continuing today, conceives and projects from the cerebral cortex of the brain a first father god.

Many humans will then compete to be closer to and to imitate the god or his instructions. Thinking to be close to the human-like origin of existence is to be favored, protected, uplifted, and unburdened by circumstances.

A human-like companion is imagined as standing above the contest of life, rooting for the humans he created to do well. Those who come in first in the busy race through life, will be more like the first father god. In terms of accomplishment, first is best, as a first father is ahead of all other later inferior fathers. A first place winner is ahead of many other losers. Life is a never ending problem, a rush and a race to obtain pleasures and to avoid pains, a situation revealed by the emphasis on progress and the continual efforts to improve conditions. Life is what it is.

To imagine a human-like god is a simplistic way of obtaining a metaphysical answer of what exists beyond the physical. The genealogical beginning of humans is made apparent by conceiving it to be a parent. Affection for an originating daddy-like god beginning, is a simplistic and childish way of relating with the origin of human life.

The suggestive hoary idea of a human-like god that is communicated to both children and adults resembles hypnosis. Suggestions of a human-like god occur at home through discussion, study, and blessings at mealtimes, and is further reinforced weekly during religious services. When repetitive suggestions of a human-like first father god are accepted by an individual, the person may then continue through life in a mild yet recalcitrant hypnotic-like trance of belief. Speaking of the origin of existence to be a human-like god evokes affection for the imagined parental forefather figure. The hypnotic suggestion, affection for, and fixation on the subjective concept of a human-like god is further spread via testimony to other suggestible individuals by the mesmerized followers of the theistic religion.

False Memory Syndrome

The cultural tradition of a human-like god is a variation of False Memory Syndrome (FMS), a condition also known as pseudo-memory and memory distortion. Though not recognized as a mental disorder, the syndrome is defined as, "A mental condition in which an individual claims to remember experiences, often traumatic, that did not happen in reality." The false autobiographical event considered to be memory, may be caused by multiple subconscious factors and conscious self suggestion by the individual, and suggestive ideas by family members or friends, and sometimes implanted during psychotherapy.

The great problem as presented in the Garden of Eden story is sin, separation from what is good, portrayed as a human-like first father god. Separate from good, humans live a cursed life of both good and evil experiences on the earth. The Genesis story is a false and imagined remembrance of a human-like first father god accepted to be true and real.

The Genesis story is not written in the first person singular tense. For example, the opening sentence of Genesis reads, "In the beginning, god created the heaven and the earth." Yet there is no mention of humans around at the time to observe the god making the universe, earth, and life, until the end of chapter one. The first verse does not read, "In the beginning I created the heaven and the earth." The only other feasible explanation is that the chapter and those that follow are written by a person or persons who artistically created the portrayed events.

For most humans, remembering a biological father, a grandfather, and perhaps a great grandfather, is the limit of individual memory. Only stories based on tradition and memories are passed down about family forefathers. Thinking about the progression of many fathers, the Jews took an extra extreme step to the genealogical terminus of a first father. So began the tradition of promoting a false memory to be a human-like god. The false memory was accepted over time as real and eventually artistically memorialized, not by visual painting or sculpture but through a word portrait of story about a first father beginning.

The first few Genesis chapters are presented to be a memory and portrayed as human remembrances of past events. Yet the collective authors of the Genesis chapters are writing about events that did not actually happen in reality. The words are a composed artistic narrative that is fictional and therefore false. The story is presented as a true account of memory when in reality Genesis is an artistic contrived story. The fictional story is passed along as true by tradition, yet is truly an instance of false memory syndrome.

Jews, Christians, and Muslims, accept the words of the Genesis Garden of Eden story as historical and true, and that it is based on remembrance of actual events. Yet the event of Genesis is a false memory that never actually occurred except in artistic imagination and told as story.

Pain

Observed to begin in childhood, humans have the ability to lie. Most people are liars, first to themselves and then to others. Humans lie about many things including how much suffering they endure in life. Failing to find a real` resolution to the pain of living, many turn to an imaginary remedy.

Only a god in the brain can relieve human pain. A human-like god is only subjectively conceived and never objectively known. An appeal to a human-like god is an imagined effort to find relief from real existential pains of living, ageing, and dying. Repetitively recalling the idea of a human-like god in thought and repetition of religious ritual, is are obsessions of theistic religion. Appealing to a human-like god is a way of reducing or avoiding pain by directing attention to the beginning of all events of the environment and life.

When young there is a seeking of enjoyment, fun, and pleasures. Too soon natural pleasures become fewer, and artificial pleasures of alcohol, drugs, and food are utilized to stave off the pains of living. Pleasures become fewer and discomfort and pains become more. Pain slowly or suddenly becomes dominant through illness, injury, loneliness, and ageing. Pain comes to more and more occlude and finally shut out many of life's pleasures until death provides final relief. C'est la vie!

Brace

The word brace is defined as, "a beam or a fastener that supports or binds with another thing, a pair, to reinforce, to prepare a position so as to be ready for impact or danger." Similarly, an imagined human-like god supports humans and fastens them to their origin. Theistic humans pair themselves with their imagined god origin that prepares and reinforces individual determination and strength to overcome shocks and dangers in life.

Humans prepare for change and brace themselves against what can injure or remove them from existence, such as harmful events in the environment and the behavior of fellow humans. For safety, humans fasten themselves to a human-like god and so reinforce their existence. Some brace themselves by fleeing now events, into the past, some into an imagined beginning of a first father god and the origin of all environmental and life events. Humans may also flee into the future, and look forward to being in the presence of a human-like god.

Humans seek to feel safe in a vast landscape of high mountains, an immense sky of mysterious lights, air and winds, and great rivers and oceans. Humankind does not have experience of and consequently does not know of anything greater than the real environment. Humans can only imagine something to be as great or to be greater than the environment by imagining a personality of a human-like god. By use of imagination then, humans increase their small stature in the greater environment. Theists ameliorate their nonspecial and inferior status by imagining their origin to be an always existing and special first father god.

An imagined human-like god conceals the truth of human life and is therefore an untruth. The biblical story of a human-like first father god is inferior human knowledge for the beginning of the environment and life. The story is a human way to be narcissistically special and superior to both the environment and all other life forms. From moment to moment, each individual human struggles to reduce limiting pains and to obtain pleasure, and a god is imagined and relied upon to see the personal plight and to render help.

Tragic Farce

While attending the 2008 Holocaust Educational Trust dinner meeting in London, concentration camp survivor and author Elie Weisel (1928-present) is said to have declared that he personally witnessed three people who actually put the Jewish god on trial in the Auschwitz concentration camp during World War II. When a few people at the dinner doubted him, Weisel replied:

"I was the only one there. It happened at night; there were just three people. At the end of the trial, they used the word chayav…it means, he owes us something. Then we went to pray."

Those at the covert hushed meeting found the god to be "chayav," meaning the god committed a transgression, he violated a law or rule by not responding and therefore is liable, he owes attention and assistance and is in debt to the Jewish people. Found to be at fault, the god only owes his people. A mild verdict considering the events of the holocaust.

Weisel then states that after finding the god at fault, those assembled then went to pray. Instead of finding the long term concept of a first father god to be at fault, and then sanely discarding it, the concept was left intact. The god was only blamed and found to be at fault and in debt to the Jewish people. Even though there was none then and there continues to be no response from the god, the artistic concept stays in place and will not be dislodged and discarded from thinking. The long established imaginary companion and habit for ritual behavior cannot be disgorged from the Jewish brain. In reality the Jews owe it to themselves to discard the imaginary companion of a human-like god.

Based on his real life experience, in the year 1977 Weisel wrote the fictional work that he refers to as a "tragic farce" entitled, *The Trial of God*. The story of prosecuting the god is set in the year 1649 during a violent pogrom against the Jewish people in Eastern Europe.

The view that there is a first father beginning is the real farce. What the Jewish people went through in Germany during World War II is tragic, yet even more tragic is the continued delusion of a human-like god who punishes them at various times for a lack of complete goodness. The Jews are separate from the goodness of the god and the goodness of the Garden of Eden. They therefore live marooned on the cursed evil earth made by the god for humans to toil upon.

In the personality of complete goodness of the ancestor god, boils up anger and curses that inflict the evils of punishment upon the Jews, or their god refuses to rescue them. The complete goodness of the god inflicts punishment of diseases, disasters, and enemies. The god is therefore not complete goodness as he ironically dispenses evils as a guide to direct humans to his goodness. The god punishes the Jews for their sins, their acts of separation from complete goodness. Harmful events in the environment and society are the god's punishing guide to goodness for the Jews. This warped view sees bad events as coming from the complete goodness of their ancestor origin. The haunting ambivalent obsession of a first father god is not easily escaped from by the Jews.

The Jewish cerebral cortex is guilty of wrongly conceptualizing the origin of existence. The cerebral cortex is guilty of valorizing the beginning of the environment and life by conceiving, imagining, and portraying it to be a human-like god. The Jews projected their longing to know the beginning of existence, and their longing for a protective ancestor. The Jews identified the activity of the origin of the universe to be a thinking and word-using first father god.

There is no human-like agency that dispenses good or evil. A human-like god only brings subjective and not objective relief to humans. The human-like god is only a "front man," an abstract concept for the matrix of the real energy and power of the environment, and its continuation as a triune soul force inside the living body. The term front man is defined as "A man who serves as a nominal leader but who lacks real authority or power; a figurehead, one who appears respectable for some nefarious activity."

A human-like god exists in subjective idea and name only. The god is a figure for the energy of the universe, and an antidote to the triune soul within the human body. The god is a respectable goodness for the nefarious good and evil business of life, and a front for male parental authority.

On the witness stand of life, Jewish thinkers must someday admit the truth, that the origin of existence is wrongly conceived to be human-like. All other theists must also admit their guilt and must swear to tell the truth and nothing but the truth.

The beginning of existence is not human-like and is not completely good. The motion of the universe is ever active and is continued in the motion of the earth that is continued in the motion and function of organs and cells of the human body and brain, and all of life. To artistically imagine and fashion the sculpture, painting, and word portrait of any human-like god and then to consider it to be real is a hideous error with often tragic consequences. The personality of a human-like god only represents the reasoning conscious self, the cerebral cortex of the brain as it struggles with the environment and the irrational subconscious triune soul within the individual and fellow humans.

Religion and Art

The first evidence of recognition of a human-like god occurred with the anthropomorphism of the earth to be a mother figure by Paleolithic humans circa 100,000-10,000 BCE. This is evident in the human artifact behavior of burial, making of female figures, and European cave painting.

Early humans were surely intimidated by the great size of the earth, and its many phenomena of the sky, such as stars, planets, asteroids, and comets. To feel comfortable in an alien land, humans eventually filled the great unknown with a forefather god, greater than all of the universe. As humans make tools, utensils, clothing, and buildings, so too simplistically taking themselves as a model, they fashioned a numerical first father god who made the environment and life.

Generally speaking, what magnifies a human-like god to be great, is that it is the first parent of a great many humans, as a grand and great father.

Human conscious imagination and remembrance of subconscious dreams contributed to the development of painting and sculpture of animals, humans, and eventually various gods. In historic times, the phenomenon of a childhood imaginary companion is continued in the adult ability to use abstract words and writing to artistically fashion and depict in story form an invisible human-like first father god of theism.

The average human will not easily accept the view that a human-like god is only subjectively real. The general population will continue for some time into the future to think of a human-like god as objectively real, and will steadfastly insist that a god is outside of the brain/mind. At some time in the future, humans will eventually come to accept that a human-like god is based on the childhood phenomenon of an imaginary companion and that a god is an artistic product of the human brain. While the cognitive aberration that a human-like god exists outside of the brain has certain benefits, the simplistic view of an objective god will forever remain false and foolish.

For theists, the artistic depicted word portrait of a nonvisible human-like god represents the beginning of existence. The theistic word portrait of a human-like god continues to hang in the history museum and art gallery of the human brain/mind. Yet some day, the collection will be updated, rotated, and retired from view. In place of the focal point of a word portrait of a human-like god, will be a visible portrait of the cosmos. It will perhaps be a mobile with galaxies in slow motion so as to illustrate the unseen field and ground of a cosmological force that moves all things into, through and out of existence.

Light

Early humans learned to scavenge for fire and eventually to make it.

As fire use evolved, sitting around the comfort and safety of burning flames, the outside sensations and image of it inside the human brain, sparked the desire to survive and to comprehend. Fire thereby lit and contributed to a limited yet evolving illuminating intelligence inside the human brain.

Conceived and forged in the limited and feebly lit intelligence of the human brain, a human-like god is a little light in a large cosmological darkness. The human brain is an evolved natural light of intelligence, while knowledge of a human-like god is an artificial light made by humans. The human brain found a way to illuminate the dim and darkness of life and death through the faulty imagining of a companion, a human-like first father god in a sequence of genealogical fathers. A god is a human made feeble candle, lantern, or flashlight within the brain to shine outward, utilized to ostensibly better see where the environment and life comes from, how events happen, how to behave on earth, and to shine into the unknown realm of dark death. Yet, the conceived candle of a god only subjectively illuminates the human brain and does nothing to illuminate the objective reality of environment.

Regulation

The biblical phrase the "children of Israel," occurs over six hundred times in the King James Bible. (Judges 4:1, 3) Since many children do have imaginary companions, the children of Israel are no exception, and they too en masse accepted an imaginary companion to be real. For the Israelites, the imaginary companion was a genealogical first father god. Preferring not to have a sculpture or painting of the god, they instead agreed to portray the god using a word portrait that explained the beginning of existence and also served to impose ethical commandments.

Theistic religion finds comfort in an imagined human-like god, aka the cerebral cortex of the brain that imagines and artistically portrays the beginning to be a genealogical first father. The god wants order among humans and so issues commands to be followed. A human-like god reinforces human will to survive and to succeed in life. He functions to impose an intelligent authority and order on the unintelligent disorder of the environment and human behavior.

The human-like god who is said to be endowed with an unencumbered free will, did not curse the first humans but he wanted to punish them as a way of regulating their behavior. In reality, biological life is a punishment of continual adjustment to conditions.

God, government, science, and the environment regulate human behavior. The conscious self or cerebral cortex imagines a human-like god to regulate behavior. Government laws impose punishment based on the criteria of what a "reasonable person" with an unimpaired conscious cerebral cortex will do in any situation. Modern science relies on the conscious cerebral cortex to measure and invent pragmatic comforts. Since life is supported by and is a continuation of the earth, the environment regulates both conscious and subconscious biological behavior. The environment is the great primal regulator of biological life.

Pragmatic Metaphor

Evolving human intelligence invents and makes tools, weapons, shelters, clothing, and ornaments. Yet, to better survive, some humans need an increase of intelligence and since this cannot be accomplished quickly in reality, inventive humans use imagination to make the pragmatic cognitive tool of a human-like first father god.

The biblical Garden of Eden story characters of Adam and Eve are simplistic and unintended metaphors of psychological and physiological reality experience. The conscious cerebral cortex represents its own presence as an imagined intelligent first father god. The comparatively small cerebral cortex presents the larger subconscious cerebellum, midbrain, and body, as the much less intelligent and disobedient first humans. With the imagined assistance of a human-like god, the cerebral cortex seeks to command and control both the environment and the disobedient urges of the cerebellum, midbrain, and body. The smaller conscious reasoning part of the brain opposes the much larger subconscious non-reasoning brain and body.

What theists worship as a human-like god, is in reality the worship of the egocentric cerebral cortex.

In imagination, the god will save humans from the outside environment, other life forms, and fellow humans. The god will also save humans from the curse of a disobedient triune soul force that forces life to live as hunger for food, sex and reproduction, and aggression. The meager intelligence of the cerebral cortex conceives, projects, and seeks protection in life, and to be rewarded in an afterlife dimension by basking in the conceived higher intelligence of a human-like god.

Humans are conditioned to act as they do in subconscious obedience of the body to the environment, not to a human-like god. The cerebral cortex brain fabrication of a human-like god is a contrived way of obtaining and enforcing obedience to authority and to maintain group order. A human-like first father god who made everything, is a symbol of filial piety and a rally point to meet and to imaginatively face a shared origin of mutual kinship.

Separation

The Garden of Eden story of sin as a separation between a first father god and humans is a metaphor that represents the physiological experience of puberty, and differing functions of the brain. With the onset of both male and female puberty, there is an increase of willfulness and disobedience to parental authority. The portrayed original sin of separation from an artistically imagined human-like god, is in reality a portrayal of individual separation from real parental authority and order. Hunger for food, sex and reproduction, and aggression overthrow both outside parental authority and easily overthrow the inside authority of the cerebral cortex. The sin of separation is also that of the individual conscious cerebral cortex from the subconscious cerebellum, midbrain, and body functions.

The great separation from goodness is imagining it to be the parental authority of a human-like first father god. In reality, only the good and evil of the real environment and life experience exists. All of the words of theological texts ever written, and the words of theologians St Augustine, St Thomas Aquinas, and many others, discuss mere metaphors.

The theology of a human-like god is only a simple patent metaphor, mere collections of an imagined artistic word portrait for the real dynamic of human behavior and biological experience.

Lie and Truth

A good god is an imagined guide to the goodness of a known beginning and protection from harm. To do evil and to disobey is to sin, to separate from goodness, to risk punishment, and to be without protection.

The sin of separation from goodness is the real biological vulnerability to pain and mortality, and to hunger for food, sex and reproduction, and aggression. Life is effort and struggle and is imagined as proceeding from the goodness of a first father god. If a father is good, and a grandfather is good to have, then the imagined idea of a first father is even better to have. If the first father made not only life but the vast environment as well, then he must not be a weak-willed human, he must be an all-powerful human-like god.

Most people lie to themselves and to others for the purpose of making themselves feel good about their individual life. This is also the case with a human-like god. The existence of a human-like god is an individual and socially acceptable lie as it contributes to a good feeling of protection from harm, the unknown, and death.

The true origin of humans can today be traced to the genitals and bodies of the parents, whose forebears like all of life evolved from the earth environment. All relative motion of the universe and function of life is a continuation of a cosmological force. A human-like god is the superficial cognitive covering over this depth of truth.

Godly Cerebral Cortex

A rather small conscious human cerebral cortex of just sixteen billion neurons must perform the Herculean task of adjusting to the outside environment and other life forms. The cortex must further adjust to the seventy billion neurons of the subconscious cerebellum and midbrain, and ten trillion cells of the body.

The conscious cerebral cortex is a mediator between the vast nonconscious earth environment, and the subconscious function of the cerebellum, midbrain, and body.

An individual does not have to go very far to experience a human-like god. The god is located quite close by, within the human brain. If a person could peer into their own cerebral cortex, they would soon find the concept of a human-like god located there. The imagined companion of a human-like god is in reality a dependence on what is higher in fellow humans, the cerebral cortex of the brain.

An imagined, observant, parental god is a way of mediating human behavior toward each other for the better. The worst interpersonal behaviors are those of the cerebellum, midbrain, and body functions of a triune soul force. The imagined devil of life is the real evils of killing and eating food, sex and reproduction, and aggression. The conscious cerebral cortex can reason and care for others, while the subconscious cerebellum, midbrain, and body function for individual survival, and are nonreasoning and generally uncaring.

The conception of a human-like intelligent god represents the conscious cerebral cortex of the human brain. An external god is preferred by some humans to be the origin of life over the environment and the internal subconscious triune soul of hunger for food, sex and reproduction, aggression. For somnambulant humankind, a dreamy allegorical story of a human-like god is preferable over an unknown beginning. For human comprehension, in the Semitic Middle East the beginning of existence is artistically depicted to be a human-like god portrayed in a Bible and Quran word portrait of obtuse contradictory scriptural writings.

The Genesis story of sin (Hebrew hata, separation) or separation from a human-like first father god and model of goodness, represents the separate function of the conscious cerebral brain from the dominate subconscious midbrain and body functions that cannot possibly be conscious or reasonable. An ethical separation is represented in the Garden of Eden story between a human-like first father god and the first man and woman.

What the story represents is that the cerebellum, midbrain, and body are separate from and cannot function like the higher functions of the cerebrum or cerebral cortex.

In the biblical Garden of Eden story, a human-like god uses only good thoughts and words to create a universe and life. He soon used bad thoughts and words to curse the first humans. Sex and reproduction then became an inferior and bad way of creating life. This metaphorical scenario is in reality, the smaller intelligent conscious cerebral cortex consciously judging the larger less intelligent subconscious parts of the brain, the cerebellum and midbrain, and the cellular mass of the body.

The intelligent human cerebral cortex makes an intelligent human-like god in its own image. The higher positioned and evolved intelligence of the cerebral cortex sees the good and evil of life experience, the hazards and dangers of the environment, and seeks to escape it by imagining and artistically crafting an intelligent human-like god. The conscious cerebral cortex also observes and is appalled by the compelling and forceful subconscious urges within the midbrain and body that act to preserve life. The human cerebral cortex then seeks a way out by imagining the origin of life to be a caring first father god.

Not knowing reasonably like the cerebral cortex, the subconscious cerebellum, midbrain, and autonomic nervous system knows only unreasonable hunger for food, sex and reproduction, and aggression. The subconscious demands the conscious cerebral cortex devise a means to obtain what is needed. This is the will to live of the subconscious triune soul that forces life to live and survive.

The boxer Mike Tyson (1966-present) commented about other boxers, "Everybody has a plan until they get hit in the face." In other words, the reasoning cerebral cortex of the brain is only effective to a limit; nonreasoning sufficient aggression of the body must then be exerted to conclude the boxing contest.

The physiological reality is that the conscious cerebral cortex and central nervous system find it difficult to direct the subconscious cerebellum, midbrain, and the autonomic nervous system of the body. While modified by conscious knowledge, the subconscious triune soul reigns supreme over conscious reasoning. The subconscious triune soul that forces life to live as hunger for food, sex and reproduction, and aggression, dominates the reasoning and measuring ability of making tools, and the ability to measurably adjust to human ethical situations of right and wrong and good and bad. The difficulty of ethical behavior is in part why a human-like first father god companion is imagined and artistically crafted into a word portrait in the theistic scriptures of Judaism, Christianity, and Islam.

The relatively small human cerebral cortex artistically imagines a much larger knowing human-like god to dangle over earthly experience of life and death. This is a strategy of projecting and magnifying the evolved innate conscience of the human cerebral cortex, to be an imagined greater spectator of a human-like first father god. The disparity between the cerebral cortex and the cerebellum, midbrain, and body, is also reflected in society. Like the cerebral cortex, the intelligent minority of society excels in reasoning and success, while like the subconscious cerebellum, midbrain, and body, the socially under educated majority populace reasons little and mostly not at all, and yet exerts a major determining influence.

A human-like first father god is a simplistic and therefore most popular way to identify the origin of existence. A genealogical first father god is also pragmatically utilized as a greater social judge of individuals in the theistic society. The human-like god of popular theism is an unthinking and superficial verbal way of identifying human origin. In reality, the origin of humans is the outside environment, and the inside triune soul force that forces life to live as hunger for food, sex and reproduction, and aggression.

The artistic word crafted fictional story of a human-like god and the fist humans in the biblical Genesis story, is a feeble attempt to portray a real internal conflict between the evolved cerebral cortex, and the cerebellum, midbrain, autonomic nervous system, and cells and organs of the body. The conscious cerebral cortex artistically externalizes its origin to be a knowing human-like good god, and the subconscious cerebellum, midbrain, and body functions are deemed to be a curse from the god. The mythically imagined disobedience and separation portrayed in story, is in reality not between a first father god and humans but between the conscious cerebral cortex and the subconscious cerebellum, midbrain, and body.

A human-like god is conceived in, by, and for the cerebral cortex of the brain. The evolved cerebral cortex imposes order by identifying the origin of existence to be a human-like god as a way of reducing existential fear and uncertainty of life. The evolved cortex of the brain also imposes social order by manufacturing a caring and helping presence for humans. A human-like god is a way of rationalizing, of making rational goodness from the irrational evil of excessive force existent both outside in the environment and inside of life forms. A conceived god functions as a mediate protection from the outside environment, and from the inside triune soul force that forces life to live.

Biblical portrayed sin is also separation from many forefathers that are condensed into a human-like numerical first father god. A good god represents a genealogical line of many forefathers that must have voiced disapproval, as all later historic fathers have, of the not so good of life as hunger for food, sex and reproduction, and aggression. This is the innate dynamic of the triune soul and human behavior.

For many, contemplating the imagined and artistic idea of an objective human-like god who can intervene in life and death, is in reality a subjective comfort. Only by conceiving of a genealogical beginning can the cerebral cortex imagine its way to personal security. Scientific reasoning is a recent and real human evolved ability to measure and shape a more protective reality.

A conceived notion of a human-like first father god as the beginning of the environment and life is an immature and mistaken idea. To have faith (Latin fides, trust) in such a bizarre idea is truly a distortion of thinking. Yet the imagined and artistically modeled god continues to be needed as it is difficult to have faith and trust in fellow humans, and in one's own conscious self and problematic subconscious soul.

The word god is a simplistic way of identifying the beginning of existence and also of promoting unity among individuals. The vast majority of humans are simply too busy, unthinking, and under educated. Blind faith and dumb trust in the delivered message of a human-like god by religious authority figures is uncritically accepted. To get a social group to follow laws and to accept others is difficult for even secular governments to accomplish. A better model of authority is needed rather than a mere human, or even worse, to rely on one's own sinful separate self. It is difficult and often impossible to have faith and trust in another human or oneself. Better to have faith in and trust an all-powerful human-like first father as the beginning of the environment and life. Better an abstract model god not open to inspection and criticisms as are humans. Mere faith in a distant ideal model of good, functions best for human purposes.

Mental Model

All gods are a continuation of an innate developmental cognitive childhood ability to have an imaginary companion that is continued into immature adulthood. Imaginative ability is the basis of art, of imagining and drawing, painting, sculpting, crafting, and the use of words to describe a genealogical origin to be a first father god. Therefore, the thinking of theistic religion has for its basis, only childish immaturity and artistic imagination.

Research has found that more female children have an imaginary companion than do male children. Studies show that a higher number of women attend religious services than do men. Women are more passive and obedient and less oriented to muscular conflict as are males.

Women are therefore more generally susceptible and prone to acceptance of an imagined parental first father god figure. Males also promote male gods to shore up their authority over women.

When the reasoning of both genders is overwhelmed by outside or inside conditions, it may appeal to an imagined greater reasoning of a human-like numerical first father god who made life. The mental model of a human-like god represents and explains the beginning of the environment and life. A human-like god is also a mental model of goodness to turn to during good and evil life experiences. The god is thanked for the good and for the avoidance and relief of all too prevalent evil experience. The human-like god is an imagined model of parental protection and an authority for tradition and moral customs. The utilitarian mental model is devised and fashioned from genealogical ancestor fathers to be the very first father beginning. The imagined and artistically fashioned mental model in the brain is also a talisman and barrier to protect humans from the environment.

Rather than a human-like god being worshipped, in reality the cerebral cortex of the human brain should be revered for artistically fashioning, albeit erroneously, the pragmatic mental model of a first father god for care and protection. The human-like god is a simplistic way of identifying an unknown beginning for the average human being. No study or deeper thinking is required, only faith and trust that theistic authorities are correct.

Religious faith and trust is directed to an objective human-like god. When a person has subjective faith in a human-like god, in reality they have faith in a psychological projection of the cerebral cortex of the human brain that fashions an artistic model of the beginning and of human care. Yet the small conscious cerebral cortex is secondary to the larger primary subconscious cerebellum, midbrain, and body cells and organs.

Due to an antagonistic environment, harmful life forms, other humans, and the subconscious animating triune soul, the immature cerebral cortex of western culture projects an imaginary companion of a human-like god, and accepts a word portrait of it sketched by Middle Eastern theistic mythic religious scriptures.

In the twenty-first century, the artistic model of a human-like god will increasingly deteriorate into a mottled and shabby condition. The painted concepts and word portrait of the mental model of a human-like first father god are continuing to fade, peel, and fall away from the human brain/mind.

Contrast

In the biblical Garden of Eden story, Jewish myopic thinking sees human life to be cursed by their very own first father god. Therefore, Jewish thinking fails miserably to clearly see reality as it truly is. Not having been made with a soul, only a living body, Jews require many commandments from a human-like first father god to curb their behaviors. The Jewish male god is a patriarchal commander who imposes many commandments on his people. The patriarchal commandments are needed to control human behavior portrayed as sinfully separating, caused by eating a forbidden fruit in an act of disobedience.

What a contrast, a patriarchal Jewish god, and the projected yet clear sighted Hindu artistic model of a god that correctly mirrors the triune soul. The Hindu male god Shiva is represented by the sculpture of the lingam-yoni, the human male and female genitals. Shiva is also known as the destroyer, and Lord of the cosmic dance, of bringing all things into existence and then for them to go out of existence. The god Shiva reflects the soul of life, sex and reproduction, aggression, both activities of which require food. The god Shiva is an artistic yet correct model correspondence with the triune soul of life. For Shiva, the cause and effect change of karma is sufficient and real to guide humans through life and death. No artistically imagined god is required to oversee or to reward and punish human behavior.

Soul

There is a supernatural beginning of the natural environment and life, yet it is not human-like in any way. That which moves within physical life is a metaphysical force that is a continuation of a cosmological force. That which is inside of life is a continuation of that which is located outside as the earth environment, elements of energy as atoms and electrons, and a cosmological force.

The beginning of life is located inside of living forms as a triune soul force of hunger for food, sex and reproduction, and aggression that forces life to live.

Humans like most living forms, stay busy in daily life by obtaining food, having sex and reproducing, and acting with verbal and/or physical aggression. This is the mostly subconscious function of the seventy billion neurons of the cerebellum, midbrain, and the one hundred trillion cells of the body that forces life to live and survive.

Humans have a further advanced activity which most other life forms do not have, measuring. This is evolved reasoning, (Latin ratio, measure) a function of the conscious cerebral cortex composed of sixteen billion neurons. Humans more so than any other known living form, like to measure space distances of height, width, and depth, and to measure time of now, past, and future. Humans investigate, explore, and measure as much as they possibly can from the largest galaxies to quantum particles, and the functions of living forms.

Making the image of a human-like god with words, is a way of measuring the unmeasurable. To extrapolate human existence back in time to a beginning and to label it as human-like is to apply a human measure to an unknown beginning. The Jewish tale that glorifies a human-like god to be the origin of life, ignores and diminishes the true cause of life, the supportive environment and the triune soul of hunger for food, sex and reproductions, and aggression.

In the biblical Garden of Eden story, a human-like god is artistically portrayed as the beginning of the environment, life, and the making of the first two humans. In reality, the triune soul force of hunger for food, sex and reproduction, and aggression, supported by the environment and as a continuation of a cosmological force, is the real maker of existence. In the story, the human-like god is artistically elevated to precedence over the animating triune soul of life that is treated as a curse by the god.

Humans consciously attempt to follow the dictions of a humanlike god but in reality only subconsciously follow the dictates of the environment. The attempt to identify the origin of existence to be a human-like first father god is an inept effort to find the animating origin of life. The origin of life is an animating triune soul force that forces life to live. It is a continuation of the energy of the environment that is a continuation of a sole cosmological force.

Yet theists do not trace the origin of life to the environment. The beginning of life is not observed to be within living forms as a continuation of the environment and a non-human-like cosmological force but is outside as an all good first father god. The triune soul of hunger for food, sex and reproduction, and aggression is overlooked to instead focus on the beginning of humans to be a human-like good first father god.

Humans like to generally think of life as good and themselves as protected. Contrary to the Genesis story, the beginning of life is not good and there is no real human-like god, only an imaginary companion. In reality, the beginning is a cosmic go continued in an environment that consists of circles of energy called elements, and is continued in the going and growing of life as a triune soul force. Both environment and life are a continuation of a cosmological force. The growth and evolving change of life is animated by a triune soul, the environment is animated by energy elements, and the animator of both is a cosmological force. This is the santana dharma, the eternal truth.

For Jews the origin of existence is an outside god that forces the environment and life into existence. For Judaism, the builder of life is exclusively outside of the body as a numerical first father god. There is no special animating force inside of humans. Jews must take a dirt nap until the biblical bookish tribal god resurrects their body from moldering remains. This way of thinking is alien to European and Indian thinking.

Contrasting the theistic imaginary companion story of existence, is that of realistically observing how life originates. Life is supported by and is a continuation of the environment.

Set within the environment, the place to observe where life comes from is inside the living body. What grows within life is an intimate continuation with an outside environment, just as the growth within the body of a unborn child is an intimate and dependent continuation with the mother. The growth of life is a continuation from where it originates.

Humans cannot consciously make their own body, yet a subconscious triune soul force can make living forms and humans. The Jews overlook the animating soul for what they conceive to be a glorified imaginary companion of a human-like first father god. The Jews saw the subconscious triune soul of hunger for food, sex and reproduction, and aggression, as a curse rather than as what animates life. This theistic error long continues to delude en masse.

In the Genesis story, short-sighted theistic Jews saw a continuing body hunger for food, sex and reproduction, and aggression to be the result of fruit ingestion. The Jews as do all theists, continue to conceive of the animating force of life to be outside of life as an external first father god. The real animating force of life is removed from inside the body and projected outside to be an imaginary companion of a human-like god. The god is also exonerated of the mess of life and honored as a great good separate from the good and evil of human life.

A human-like god is an imaginary good companion that speaks for group values and so judges whether each individual is good or bad. The insistence on, and the acceptance of a human-like forefather god, is a way of promoting obedience and insuring order by following and being under the scrutinizing gaze of an authority figure and his earthly minions. This ruse and misdirected attention to an imaginary human-like god is a way of opposing the real environment and a real triune soul that forces life to live. The biblical good god condemns humans for their evil desire for sex and reproduction, and for the excess force of aggression, and the accursed human struggle to obtain food to reduce ever recurring hunger.

The evidence is compelling, convincing, and beyond a reasonable doubt that the Jews sinned not by disobeying an imaginary first father god but by disparaging a real animating soul. The conscious cerebral cortex, alias the good god, is appalled by the subconscious cerebellum, midbrain and body functions, and responds by imagining a better beginning of a human-like god. It is also believed that since the god formed a human body once from the outside, he will, after a long dirt nap by the many deceased, reform or resurrect humans again someday in an unknown future. Mature and sane individuals and cultures must disengage from these truly ignorant ways of thinking.

The biblical story of the beginning of humans as made by a human-like first father god begins only in the human brain. A human-like god is a conceived model and symbol for a great amount of time and sequence of a great many forefathers. Both time and many human generations are collapsed down and shaped to fit inside the essence of an imaginary companion.

The fear of punishment by a human-like god is in reality a fear of what will occur next in the usually unknown cause and effect sequence and events of time. Therefore, for many, an imagined companion of a human-like first father god functions as a buffer to somewhat relieve fear of the unknown.

The glorification of a human-like super reasoning god, is humankind's imaginary way of seeking relief and to escape from the outside environment and from the inside soul. The conscious cerebral cortex seeks to at least find relief from the triune soul that forces life to live as the subconscious cerebellum, midbrain, and body. The cerebral cortex also seeks relief from an uncertain changeable environment such as weather, asteroids, and comets, thought to be thrown down upon the earth by an angry imaginary companion god.

Relief from life has long been sought by imagining a human-like numerical first father god. Only recently has the conscious cerebral cortex sought relief from the subconscious soul and the environment through the empirical sciences.

Yet just as religion has in the past, even science will find a difficult challenge to manage the subconscious triune soul as the hunger for food, sex and reproduction, and aggression that ever forces life to live and evolve.

Long Lastingness

A human-like god is a vicarious substitute for those who lack intelligence and are unable to think for themselves. There are a number of surveys and studies that convincingly show a correlation between education level and religious belief of a human-like god. The general research shows a correlation that the more education a person has, the less religious oriented they are; the less education, the more religious. Theistic religions are most popular and the masses flock to them to obtain a god who will think for them. Most humans prefer to be dependent on a human-like god rather than be a member of a religion that teaches exploratory and developmental disciplines such as meditation and yoga.

Human sin (Hebrew hata, separation) is the physiological separation of the conscious cerebral cortex of the brain from the subconscious cerebellum, midbrain, and body. The mental dynamic is that the subconscious triune soul of hunger for food, sex and reproduction, and aggression dominates the conscious self of reasoning and measuring. This physiological condition within humans is metaphorically and psychologically compensated for by imagining and projecting a human-like god that is portrayed in story and communicated to be a good entity separate from humans. A good human-like god is a proverbial carrot that keeps humans moving forward through life and inevitable death. To better observe the brain and body of the conscious self and subconscious soul is the way to gradually remove the cognitive separation.

The essence of the triune soul force as hunger for food, sex and reproduction, and aggression that forces life to live, must be reduced and guided to a better result so as to reach a favorable end of a long journey. As the cosmological force of the universe is long existent, and as the environment is long lasting, so too is the continuation and essence of a triune soul force long lasting in spite of a short lasting biological life.

The biological body is short lasting but its animating essence is long lasting. Human essence is a continuation of long lastingness.

Continuation

The thing that exists on its own, is a cosmological force, field, or ground, and is the inferred yet unseen impetus for the environment and life. From a primary cosmological force secondary particle forces of energy and forms of the environment are derived, and from this support is derived the physical force of living cell and organ functions. The triune soul force has an origin in a sequence of relative force. A powerful hunger for food, sex and reproduction, and aggression, are a continuation of a powerful environment that is a continuation of an all-powerful cosmological force.

The triune soul of hunger for food, sex and reproduction, and aggression, is an innate force to survive. The subconscious soul intrudes into conscious attention of the cerebral cortex as forceful urges to be directed, satisfied, or postponed. The subconscious cerebellum, midbrain, and body continuously, with only brief respites, disturbs and distorts conscious reasoning of the cerebral cortex. In other words, the subconscious triune soul of hunger for food, sex and reproduction, and aggression, easily intrude upon the cerebral cortex attention and reasoning activity with demands for food, sex, and aggression.

Various religions and philosophies have been correct in vaguely perceiving that something exists inside of humans and other living forms that resists destruction at the time of physical death. However, that which resists destruction is inevitably and unfortunately wrongly conceived. The soul is not made by an imagined human-like first father god but instead is a continuation of a sole cosmological force.

The conscious cerebral cortex imagines a companion and artistically fashions a word portrait story of a human-like god to save humans from life and death. In reality, the subconscious soul that forces an individual to live also saves the person from annihilation.

The cerebral cortex must also see that the triune soul force, as is all force, energy, and momentum, is conserved from one dimension to another. As a triune soul force and a sole cosmological force are identical, the duo of both subconscious and conscious willing, and at least some memory images of the brain continue beyond physical death.

Ten Commandments

The conscious cerebral cortex that consists of sixteen billion neurons, oversees and mediates for the other seventy billion brain neurons of the subconscious cerebellum and midbrain, and the one hundred trillion cells of the body. Yet, it is the seventy billion neurons of the midbrain and subconscious autonomic functions of the body that command the conscious cerebral cortex. This is why the conscious cerebral cortex fashions a human-like god, and projects a greater personality that can direct and control environmental events, and can also influence the inner conscious and subconscious behavior of humans.

The sixteen billion neurons of the cerebral cortex of the brain fashions a human-like god to reinforce its meager reasoning ability, to voice conscious concerns, and to identify its own origin. The memory of a real father and grandfather is traced back to an imagined genealogical first father god.

While six hundred and thirteen commandments are given by the Jewish human-like god through the books of the Old Testament, the Decalogue or Ten Commandments are better known. (Exodus 20; Deuteronomy 5:6-21) The first commandment recognizes a human-like god, and demands that Jews should not have any other gods before the originating first father god of his people. The Jews also sought to distance themselves from the artistic creation of the gods of other religions by the second commandment, "Thou shalt not make unto thee any graven images." Only written words are allowed to direct attention to the very first forefather of the group. While the Jewish god is like all gods, an artistic expression, the god is not artistically portrayed in visible sculpture or painting. The first father of the Jews is artistically portrayed as a word portrait in the Tanakh or Old Testament.

The third command prohibits taking the name of the god in vain. To do so would be to also criticize the genealogical line of fathers. The fourth command is to remember the Sabbath day and to keep it holy. The Sabbath is a time to remember and to imitate the first father in resting from the god's labors of making the environment and life. Obviously a human-like tribal god who tires may in a quaint way, just need some rest now and then.

The cerebral cortex of the human brain seeks to direct the subconscious behavior of the body, the triune soul force of hunger for food, sex and reproduction, and aggression. The following commandments deal with regulating acts of aggression. The fifth commandment is to honor thy father and mother, as there is a tendency by younger people to disobey, dishonor, and to aggressively disrespect parents. The sixth is to not kill, the seventh is not to commit adultery, while the eighth is to not steal. The ninth is to not bear false witness, while the tenth is to not covet a neighbor's house, wife, servant, ox, ass, or any other possession.

The commandments are an authoritative guide for individual behavior as a member of a group. The commandments are a "group think," defined as a psychological phenomenon in which individuals of a group seek for consensus and agreement among its members. Members may then suspend or ignore their own views and adopt the majority group view rather than express dissent. Fear of rejection by the group and wanting harmony among members then prevails.

Prior to Christmas time in December, parents tell their children that Santa Claus or Father Christmas is on his way to visit and will reward good boys and girls. In the same way through many years, parental theist authorities tell immature adults that a human like god is coming or at least will reward good adults and punish the bad, either on earth or when they visit the god in an afterlife dimension. As long as there exists immature and unthinking adults on the planet earth, the use of a human-like first father god as a way of knowing an unknown beginning, and to know right from wrong and will continue into the future. The idea of a human-like first father god of humankind is a subjective idea and to represent it to be an objective reality is a bona fides mistaken delusion.

Mistake

Human attention directed to the past and to a first father god is an attempt to have knowledge of the origin of life, and is also a way to have protection and to avoid the hazards of living and the oblivion of death. To identify the origin of life to be a human-like god is a clumsy and defective way of expressing a relative relationship with an animating force. Yet the thoughts and emotions of many humans continue to cling to the long conceived and accepted idea.

A human-like god is the colossal ego of humans, a blown out of proportion primitive strategy to identify the origin of existence, and a way of feeling better about the suffering of life, ageing, and death. Faulty human intelligence mistakenly identifies a first father intelligence to be the origin of the environment and life. A human-like first father god is imagined to overlook the earth and an afterlife dimension. Theism is a human mistake, defined as "an error or fault resulting from defective knowledge or carelessness in identifying a situation incorrectly or wrongly." Evolving human intelligence identified and placed the origin of existence in the wrong place. Theism is an astigmatic aberration, a mistake, an error in judgment, and a long term delusion of humankind.

Theism is a sin, a separating mistake of human intelligence that narcisstically insists the origin of life is a greater human-like intelligent god. Theism is a futile attempt by the conscious cerebral cortex to identify the unknown origin of life, mistakenly assumed to be a human-like first father god. Truth is to illuminate the dark mistake of theism and its human-like god of Judaism, Christianity, and Islam. In reality, an artificial and false god is substituted for the truth that the origin of life is inside of it as a triune soul that is a continuation of the environment and a cosmological force. Attention to a human-like god bypasses what is inside of humans that animates life, a triune soul force of hunger for food, sex and reproduction, and aggression that forces life to live. Life is a continuation of the environment, and a continuation of a cosmological force that forces the cosmos to be in motion.

Time

All too often vulnerable and helpless, humans become willfully stubborn in particular situations. Stubbornness easily progresses to stupidity. In an attempt to find stability in the continual change of living, humans often stubbornly persist in a course of action. The momentum of the insisted on behavior gives meaning to what of necessity must change and so the endeavor is eventually rendered a futile effort.

Conscious effort attempts to override or control the conditions of the outside environment and the inside subconscious triune soul. Eventually an individual has to realistically accept the more powerful conditioning of the environment and the directing presence of the triune soul. It is the nonconscious environment and the subconscious soul that conditions and controls each conscious individual.

Infinite space and time is punctuated by an imagined human-like god. Seeking control of the environment and individual life, humans inwardly imagine and then project outward a human-like god. A human-like god is the human imaginative attempt to reinforce personal individual efforts. A god is the timeless hope of humans to control the unceasing change and events of a lifetime, ageing, and death.

Infinite time as Kronos and Saturn devour and swallow all things of the environment and life. Evanescent moments of now and what is, transit forevermore to the great reservoir of what was and has been. Bobbing in the vast ocean of time, an immense spatial environment, and the subconscious soul inside, each person looks for a preserver to avoid drowning in an uncertain environment, and sinking into the abyss of the subconscious. Humans seek to preserve themselves by grasping at passing preservers of food, sex and reproduction, and aggression, and the everyday life preservers of interests and goals, held to for a brief time on the tossing cosmic sea of living and dying. An imagined human-like god bestows a super meaning to an all too often disappointing and less than meaningful life.

So that continual change does not submerge and swallow up an individual, a goodly number look to a human-like god to save them from the ravages of time. An imagined human-like god is a way of not being forgotten by the origin of existence, of being remembered. A human-like god is said to be endowed with super memory and can keep track of all the events of an individual life so that voracious time does not destroy and reduce it to total oblivion. While mortal humans will forget through time and ageing, a super human-like god will never forget to care for an individual.

Dismayed and depressed by the death and decay of the body, it is popularly thought that only the beginning of a human-like god can at some time in the future resurrect the body. This is wishful theistic thinking. In reality, a human-like god will never save a human. Only the subjective idea of a god will save from worry, anxiety, and stress of living, ageing, and dying. An imagined human-like god does not protect an individual from disappearing into the vastness of time and death. The real savior is the triune soul. Yet the savior soul is not all powerful enough to save the body from perishing but as a continuation of energy and force is saved to another dimension. The only and real power of the soul is its resistance to destruction through time.

True Genesis

Humans witness the ceaseless changing of life and the environment and to prevent disorientation imagine a stable human-like beginning. Humans have long fawned over their origin, imagined to be a human-like first father god. In reality, humans have coevolved with the environment and other life forms, and all are a continuation of the environment. The biological body is rooted in the elements and molecules of the earth while the triune soul of life is a continuation of and rooted in a cosmological force. A cosmological force that exists on its own, brings the evolving motion of the environment into existence, and the earth brings forth the growing and evolving of life.

An aware person senses or feels there exists within their conscious self, a subconscious function as a presence that conscious attention cannot control.

This subconscious presence is the difficult to control triune soul, as hunger for food, sex and reproduction, and aggression that forces life to live.

All comes from a single unreasoning and unmeasurable and therefore irrational cosmological force, field, or ground that exists on its own. Life is irrational as it has an irrational origin from what is unhuman and unlike life. The origin of the environment and life is unlike either the earth or humans. Primitive humans of the past and theists of modern times think that only from a human-like maker can come the environment, life, and humans. This is immature kindergarten thinking by a long parade of planetary theists.

The biological body consists of particles, elements, and molecules from the earth and the stars, while the soul is a continuation of a cosmological force and is therefore resistant to destruction. It is the triune soul that forces life to live on its dimensional journey through a space and time reality.

Animating Force

A single cosmological animating force furnishes support and momentum for the relative motion of the environment and is continued in living forms as an animating triune soul force that forces life to live as hunger for food, sex and reproduction, and aggression. All is a continuation of a cosmological force and nothing can ever be separate from it.

As a continuation of a cosmological force, the physical evolution of microorganisms, plants, animals, and humans is not exclusively accomplished by the outside environment but is also on the inside by the triune soul. In humans the subconscious soul force organizes and evolves the brain cerebellum, midbrain, and organs of the body.

The subconscious autonomic nervous system of the body is juxtaposed by the conscious cerebral cortex that makes picture images of the environment and other living forms.

The conscious brain wills and makes picture images of now, past, or future. Calming the picture making of the conscious cerebral cortex reveals the non-picturing triune soul force of hunger for food, sex and reproduction, and aggression that forces life to live.

Enlightenment

His first name Siddhartha is apropos. Siddhi is the Hindu word for extrasensory abilities. Artha is the word for the four desirable goals of Hindu society, work skills, pleasure and enjoyment, duty and learning, and liberation from the round of life and death. Siddhartha was appropriately named by his parents at birth as someone who would work to reach his goals in life, and attain to liberation and a higher level of extrasensory insight and intuitive comprehension.

The Hindu son Siddhartha Gautama (circa 623-543 BCE) reached the zenith of comprehension of the human condition through investigating the self and soul. During his lifetime he became better known as the Buddha, the awakened one. Through a focus of disciplined attention and observation, he had to have clearly seen the conscious and subconscious functions of his brain and body, and he further annunciated a method of comprehension for others to emulate. His grand accomplishment has to be the result of a long foreground of effort, as his sustained search and attainment of comprehension is seemingly preternatural. His accomplishment is astounding for the time in which he lived, and continues to be a numinous feat rarely attained through the passing centuries up to modern times.

Siddhartha's focus of attention was within and he did not appeal to an imaginary companion of a human-like god. His focus of attention was on what moved an individual on a journey through life and death. He encountered the maze of the conscious self and the powerful subconscious soul, and eventually comprehended them fully.

He accomplished this feat in part by grouping the parts and functions of the body to be five. These are body, sensations, feelings, willing, and mental images and processes.

These five he confidently declared were anatma, not an eternal soul. As to what the soul actually is, he did not fully annunciate. Yet he alluded to what the soul is by emphasizing three main practices. The rule and practice of eating one meal before noon disciplines hunger for food, while the rule and practice of celibacy disciplines sex and reproduction. The discipline and practice of meditative compassion increases sensitivity and so reduces aggression.

The *Dhammapada* is a collection of sayings accepted by tradition to be the spoken words of the Buddha. The following two verses are said to have been uttered by him at the time of his awakening:

Verse 153: Through many lives I wandered, seeking but not finding the builder of this house; ill it is to be born again and again.
Verse 154: House-builder, you are seen, no house shall you build again! Rafters and ridge-pole are dismantled. My mind has reached the unconstructed; all constructing now stilled.

For Buddha, the origin of life is an internal house-builder, a correct metaphor not attributed to be outside of the body as a god. The builder of the house is the triune soul that forces the body to live, that wants to survive as hunger for food, sex and reproduction, and aggression. The builder of the house is the soul, yet the Buddha did not name it, as it is not a noun thing but a verb dynamic.

Prior to Buddha, Hindu seers correctly attributed human origin to be from the gunas or forces within the body and the environment. This recognition later contributed to the development of the five thousand year old practice of yoga breathing and body postures. Yoga is the effort to focus and control conscious attention, the picture images of now moments, past, and future, and the subconscious muscles and functions of the body. However, the Hindu tradition also made an egregious error by wrongly attributing the atma or soul to be a blissful and wonderful presence that animated the body. Hindus thought a dedicated seeker had only to uncover its transcendent glowing force.

Buddha saw not a special innate atma within the human body but a "house-builder" that builds a living house of many parts and is therefore dukkha, meaning ill-fit-together and suffering.

Life is moved by an unseen force, parts assemble and disassemble, live and die. The house-builder is also capable of continuing outside of the body, and inside another body. The builder can leave the house and build another dwelling, and like any house-builder, it has to obtain parts with which to assemble a new structure. Yet the house-builder can only use parts available, such as a fertilized egg or embryo, and cannot miraculously produce them. The triune soul force cannot start from scratch, its behavior must obey cause and effect.

Meditation Analogy

During a practice of meditation, it can be observed that conscious attention is easily pulled away from an intended focus on an object. Memories, imaginations, and associations cloud and easily sway and pull attention away from a still focus. The subconscious triune soul of hunger for food, sex and reproduction, and aggression, easily pulls and forces conscious attention away from a focus, and usurps conscious reasoning. A lack of consistent meditation practice results in an impairment to focus conscious attention.

Analogically, the clouds of conscious thoughts, memories, imaginations, and associations can be successfully cleared to reveal a luminous blue sky and a shining sun. The spatial blue sky is conscious attention for objects to appear in. The sun is in reality a burning cauldron of gases, an analogy with the heated desires of the will to live, the triune soul of hunger for food, sex and reproduction, and aggression. Unconscious sleep can be compared with the night sky of many stars that appear and the reflective light of the moon. Analogically, the stars are like dim subconscious memories and the light of the moon is semiconscious awareness of dream images.

Clearing away the obscuring clouds of conscious mental processes, reveals the subconscious soul of life to be a continuation of a nonconscious cosmological force. Then can be seen how the distorting conscious association of thoughts cloud clear seeing of the triune soul as the essence of good and evil life experiences.

The darkened subconscious function of body and cycle of habits exposed to the light of meditative attention, can be illuminated and better comprehended.

The triune soul is the essence of life and is the continuing essence in death, supported by a dimension of energy and a cosmological force. As in life the subconscious triune soul evolves and retains a surface conscious ability for thinking and reasoning. It is generally accepted by tradition that the essence of the soul is the ability to think. In reality the essence of the soul is the ability to survive.

Subject-Object

From sensations through the senses of seeing, hearing, smelling, tasting, and touching, picture images are formed in conscious attention. The outside object is pictured in the subject of conscious attention. The image of the object appears in the brain and is recognized or re-cognized as being outside the subject.

An examination of this perceptual process is ignored, caused by a twofold combination of a serial stream of conscious picture images, and emotions from the subconscious triune soul that forces life to live and to respond to hunger for food, sex and reproduction, and aggression. The conscious images are evoked and cathected with excitation by the subconscious triune soul force of hunger, sex, and aggression. An individual is torn by an ignorance of internal conscious brain and subconscious body functions, and by a struggle with outside events. The subconscious triune soul wants either to eat an object, have sex with it, or harm it. Conscious reason as the ability to measure and manipulate, has a tough task to perform.

A picture image formed in the conscious cerebral cortex of the brain, simultaneously measures an object in space and imposes a time sequence. Objects are measured in space and time by having an image of it inside the brain, and are then manipulated outside by the body.

The reality of the ocean consists of its great form, and an unseen reality of what it is composed.

Looking at the vast ocean it is difficult to discern the individual droplets of which it is composed, yet even school children know that all bodies of water consists of small drops. It is not possible to actually see with the eyes that the drops of seawater further consist of atoms and electrons that compose the H2O of water. If school children and adults are further educated in basic chemistry and physics, then the reality of the essence of the ocean can be visualized and comprehended.

Similarly, from sensations a subject-object reality of human awareness develops. Out of a sea of sensations, some are formed into conscious visual pictures of now, past, and future. To observe only pure sensations is most difficult to do. To meditatively observe the process of images forming out of the great sea of sensations is also difficult. A continual stream of picture images flows out of an ambient sea of sensations. By meditatively observing this ongoing process, relief from the dominance of conscious sensations and the image making process is accomplished.

To travel to where very few have been, is not to travel to a far destination but is to travel inside by turning attention to observing brain and body functions. Freedom from the subconscious triune soul that forces life to find food, have sex and reproduce, and to be aggressive, is most difficult. Yet there are some individuals that take on the task of self and soul comprehension to reach relief from both life and death.

Meditation

For children and many adults, there is a lack of awareness of mental processes occurring within the brain/mind. A child and an immature adult considers only physical objects as real. The ability for introspective examination and meditation does not occur naturally in adults and what is most real is the physical body. The main focus of attention of the average adult is on physical forms that probably occurs as a result of satisfying needs in the environment.

Individuals fail to comprehend that images form from sensations.

For the average human, unfocused attention fails to observe changing sensations, and fails to observe changing picture images of now, past, and future occurring in the brain. Imagination is the human ability of the brain to generate images, consciously while awake and subconsciously during sleep and dreaming. From sensations, humans generate images of time, as now, past, and future. Brain/mind attention is socially conditioned to associate, not to concentrate.

Meditation is the concentrated effort to develop an increase of ability to observe conscious mental picture images of space-time. Meditation is also training attention to observe conscious willing that is a reflection of the subconscious triune soul that forces the body to live, as hunger for food, sex and reproduction, and aggression. Effort must be used to moderately nudge and push the triune soul to eventually discipline it to a balanced state. Love as an evolute of sex, must moderate the force of aggression, and must moderate the force of hunger that enables and supports life.

Having the luxury of privacy is best for the purpose of meditation and self and soul exploration. With consistent practice develops a taming of the real essence of life, a triune soul force that forces the body to live. In this way the soul becomes self-contained, meaning, the subconscious becomes more conscious.

Undisciplined attention is an aberrant and impaired condition of disorganized brain waves. When attention is focused and stilled, an individual can better see passing now moments, what was in the past, and see what may occur in the future. Meditation can also lead to the awakening that death is a relocation of the triune soul of life to an afterlife dimension.

A beneficial method of meditation is a focus of attention on the sensation of breathing. The same shared air surrounding the earth is inhaled and exhaled by many living lungs. There is a greater invisible air surrounding the earth, and individual felt breaths of air. There exists likewise a greater nonvisible cosmological force outside of humans and a nonvisible yet intensely felt animating triune soul inside of humans that forces life to live.

By closing the eyes and retiring to a quiet place, an individual can better focus attention on the sensation of breathing. By this practice a surrender of paying attention to sensations outside the body occurs. Focusing attention on sensations of breathing, reduces and surrenders attention to picture images of now, past, and future. To calm the triune soul that forces life to live, meditation reduces and surrenders over-attention to food, to sex and reproduction, and over-attention to aggression.

With practice, attention withdraws from continual restless effort and distractions, to find relief nestled in a rarely perceived place just between subject and object. Having no partiality for either subject or object, attention free floats to apperceive its own true form and home. Effort relaxes in directing attention to either subject or object and rests free. Resting between subject and object, for moments poised free, recognizing its own pristine presence. When the sun shines where there is no object, there exist no shadows of darkness to obscure.

Soul Cluster Behavior

A sole cosmological force that exists on its own is the ground that animates the seeds of energy particles that cluster into the elements and nascent roots of the environment, and supports the clustering stem and active growth of living forms. A sole cosmological force continues inside living forms as a triune soul that forces the body to live by hungering for food, sex and reproduction, and aggression.

The word cluster is defined as, "an aggregate of parts, a number of similar things grouped, fastened, held, bunched, or growing together." Clustering is the prevalent behavior of reality. All things cluster as an assembly of relative parts. The behavior of a sole cosmological force is to emit (send out, radiate, discharge, release, and express) energy particles that cluster as varying forms and behaviors of the environment. Energy particles cluster to structure elements, in turn elements cluster to form the environment. The elements of the environment support the clustering growth and evolution of living cells. Cells of life cluster to form organs, and a living body. Living species cluster in groups in a geographical area.

Not at all human-like but perhaps with a modicum of exuberance, energy particles burst forth from a sole cosmological force, not as a Big Bang but as a Big Burst. Space is the non-appearing ground of cosmological force while time is the relative motion of environmental and living forms. An omnipresent force field forms the numberless clusters of quantum particles, atoms, and electrons. Energy particles cluster to form elements that cluster to form coherent gases, liquids, and solid forms of the environment. Environmental energy particles also cluster to construct and evolve molecular living forms. Life is a continuation of environmental energy that is traced to a cosmological force or ground.

As a continuation of a cosmological force, the triune soul forces the biological body to live, and consists of subconscious neuronal clusters of willing to obtain food, obtain sex and reproduce children, and exhibit aggression. Speculatively, the soul is a triune force, and exists as a cluster pattern of force. As in life so in death, the soul is mostly subconscious but is also conscious. The triune soul forces life to live by subconsciously and consciously hungering for food, sex and reproduction, and aggression.

The soul is a cluster pattern of willing force located in the brain and body, located in the relative energy elements of atoms and electrons of the earth, located in a greater environment of the universe, all located in a ground of cosmological force that exists on its own.

The nucleus of the soul is the triune forceful willing for food, sex and reproduction, and aggression. As a continuation of the energy elements of the earth and a cosmological force, the soul force coheres as a cluster of coherence. Consciousness or subject-object knowing, is preserved through picture images, stored as in a physical brain, as a surface concomitant to the essence of willing force.

At the time of death, the cluster of biological body cells fall away, yet as a continuation of a cosmological force, the clustering particles of energy tend to exhibit coherence and are conserved. Death is a shift from a biological cluster of cells to a cluster pattern of willing force that is anchored and rooted in an unseen dimension of cosmological force.

The biological body of cells and organs un-cluster or disassemble in death. Yet that which forces life to live and survive is a triune soul of forceful willing for food, sex and reproduction, and aggression that unless disciplined and resolved, continues to exist and recur. There is no room in a cause and effect sequence for a human-like god. All of life has a direction, propelled by its own cluster pattern of a triune soul force.

Gender and Soul

The triune soul of hunger for food, sex and reproduction, and aggression, is expressed differently in the two genders. The differing expressions are of course complimentary. The predominant expressions for women are sex and reproduction and the nursing of infant life, and gathering and preparation of food. Aggression is existent but less prominent in women. In contrast, the predominant expression for men is weighted toward aggression of offense and defense, toward obtaining food or money to buy food. Sex and reproduction is just slightly less in priority.

Male and female support each other on the soul level. Both rely on each other to obtain food and to prepare it. Both rely on each other for sexual satisfaction and for mutual support in the likely reproduction of children. Both rely on the aggression of each other in obtaining and retaining money to be used for security, shelter, and safety.

For the soul all is acceptable in the obtaining of food, sex and reproduction, and aggression. An adult imaginary companion of a human-like god is a collective way of judging this individual activity, and of directing human behavior to a better level of conscience and cooperation.

Pleasure and Discipline

An individual who addicts body and brain to alcohol, drugs, tobacco, food, or another person, attempts to stay in a temporary state of pleasure and to avoid the pain of not having, or to escape from what is unwanted.

Continually wanting to obtain or to stay in an experience of pleasure and to avoid pain is exhausting. Frustrated and progressing to exhaustion, some turn to a human-like god as a subjective mental anodyne, an antidote that brings relief from seeing and experiencing the worst of what life offers. An imaginary companion of a god is a switch of attention from the worst to that which offers relief from experiencing or seeing the suffering of life to what can assist.

The traditional ways of seeking for a human-like god, such as celibacy, fasting, solitude, prayer or meditation, is in reality disciplining the soul. The lives of humans are directed not by a human-like god but by a triune soul that forces life to live, in turn directed by the environment, in turn a continuation of a cosmological force.

Lacking discipline and training, the average person experiences that it is difficult if not impossible to consciously direct hunger for food, sex and reproduction, and aggression, Mild asceticism is a discipline in not wanting to over participate in the pleasures of life that have a tendency to lead to stress and suffering. Fasting is a way of disciplining the triune soul, of hunger for food, sex and reproduction, and aggression. Those seeking a god, often do so by abstinence from sex.

Searching for a human-like god, an individual has to meditatively reduce distraction of attention to external sensations, to observe the making of picture images, the making of a metaphorical human-like god, and to arrive at the soul that forces life to live. To reclaim a projected god-like status, humans must learn and must increase intuitive levels of comprehension, of both conscious and subconscious experience of living.

What drives conscious life through the sequential change of time, is a non-conscious movement of the environment that is continued inside of life as a triune soul force. A single living bacteria moves as a changing continuation of the supporting changing elements of the environment, earth, water, air, and photons of light and temperature. What forces the human body to consciously function, behave, and rationally think, is the subconscious irrational soul of hunger, sex, and aggression.

Humans are often helpless and imagined help is better than no help at all. Higher reasoning and intuition of the human cerebral cortex is the god. Reasoning is supported by the soul function of cells and organs of the body, as a continuation of the environment, and a continuation of a cosmological force that exists on its own.

A human-like god is an imagined way of finding relief from the environment and from the triune soul. A psychologically conceived human-like god is a way of inspiring personal confidence during chaotic struggles with the environment and other humans, and also contributes to ethics by judging human behaviors and rewarding or punishing them. Invoking a human-like god is a way of promoting unity by having a shared first father figure. The communication of any human-like god to humans, is in reality only a message in writing from a theistic human to potential other theists.

Time

The basis of existence is a cosmological force to which all is tied as all-powerful time. From a cosmological non-phenomenal and non-experienced force, flows dimensions and changing forms of time to eventually return to their origin. The basis of human conscious experience, is all-powerful time, and a triune soul force of hunger for food, sex and reproduction, and aggression.

A human-like god is a mentally constructed shelter from life on the earth, and a shelter from fear of what is anticipated after death. A human-like god is an external refuge from an all directing time that brings good things into existence yet soon changes to subtract them from an individual life and all too often adds lingering bad things. Not a human-like god but all-powerful cosmic time is what holds each in a sequence of energy and particle change. The small Jewish culture, as did its Christian and Islamic sects, have made a grievous error in anthropomorphizing time to be a human-like numerical first father god. The Semitic god is in reality an offspring of the human brain and of all-mighty ancient Kronos.

There is no first father directing the sequence of all-changing time that both relents and is unrelenting.

Unrelenting is fate while seemingly relenting is imagined to be a numerical first father god who loosens his all mighty tight grip on changes to an individual life. There is no father time but time that fathers all. The metaphorical fathering origin of relative time is in reality an un-fathered cosmological force to which all is tied. The Jews anthropomorphized time as a childish and sycophantic way to please and to appeal to a human-like first father god. The god can provide the good of pleasure and help to avoid the pain of evil or excessive force of the environment, microorganisms, animals, and fellow humans.

Spinning

A cosmological force spins all into existence. From the spinning of subatomic quantum particles and atoms and electrons, the elements are born. From the spinning elements the stars, planets, and moons of galaxies are born. From the spinning earth comes the animated motion and behaviors of life and death.

Human life is a swirling spin of experiences, thoughts, emotions, memories and imaginations that often distract, stress, tire, and if in excess often disorient individuals. Sleep provides some relief from the spinning circles of thoughts, memories, imaginations, and behaviors, as the minutes, hours, days and nights spin by without letup. Meditation practice slows the continual spinning of conscious thoughts and behaviors, to better see the conscious and subconscious springs of behavior.

The spinning experiences of life and death on earth extend to other ethereal dimensions, and to an unspun cosmological force that sets all in spinning motion. From an unspun force comes the spinning environment from which spins the daily and nightly activity of life. Set spinning by environment, the inside spinning of a triune soul, spins life experiences on earth to continue spinning thereafter, and perhaps a spinning cycle of return or reincarnation.

Conscious attention to sensations from outside and inside, and picture images of now, past, and future, are set spinning by the subconscious triune soul of hunger for food, sex and reproduction, and aggression. The outside environment churns life as does the triune soul inside. The churning and spinning of life must be meditatively observed, slowed, and comprehended. The enthusiasm for the miasma of life is to be calmed.

For humans there is a spinning changing of thoughts, memories, and imaginations. Human imagination has spun the yarn of a human-like god to control the changing and spinning physical and mental experiences of life. The Jews could not accept coming from the biological body traced back through a long line of biological births evolved from the earth. For the Jews the beginning of life came not from a greater long biological line of womb openings but came from the abruptly opened mouth of a human-like god.

Substrate

In metaphysics, the Greek word, hypokeimenon means "beneath, or what is underlying." The Latin word is substratum or substrata, defined as "a layer located beneath another layer, a basis or foundation." The English word substrate is defined as, "the nonliving surface or medium on which an organism grows from or is attached to." A substrate is that which underlies the change of forms in the universe, and is also that which persists in an object that changes. The philosopher Immanuel Kant (1724-1804) referred to the substrate of reality as the noumenon, the "thing in itself" that can be apprehended only by intuition but not known. Noumena is the opposite of phenomena or what appears and that can be known and measured.

Thoughts occur in the substrate of the brain that exists in the substrate of the biological body that exist on the substrate of the earth surface and environment. Life and the environment exist in the substrate of the greater environment of the solar system that exists in the greater substrate of the universe, to exist in the underlying substrate of a cosmological force or ground that exists on its own.

Can thoughts continue to exist without the substrate of brain and body? Thoughts exist in the brain that exist in the substrate and support of the body systems existing on the substrate of the earth environment whose substrate is particles of energy. Energy particles exist in the substrate of relative forces, and all exists in the substrate of a cosmological force, including the triune soul that forces life to live. Therefore, it is at least possible that thoughts grounded in energy and force may continue to exist following physical death.

Blasphemy

Blasphemy is defined as, "Contemptuous ridicule and insulting speech, writing, depiction, or behavior toward a god or religion; cursing or reviling so as to defame, deprive, or reduce sacredness." Blasphemy law pertains to laws that limit and punish individual speech, written or depicted works, and behaviors that criticize a god, religious leaders, artifacts, teachings, scriptures, and customs of a particular religion.

Some thirty-two countries have anti-blasphemy laws that make it a crime to openly criticize the concept of a human-like god, religious ideas, and practices. Blasphemy is a crime in the European countries of Austria, Denmark, Finland, Greece, Ireland, Italy, Lichtenstein, and San Marino. In the Netherlands, a blasphemy law existed until 2014 when it was repealed. The law punished an individual who publically in depiction, orally, or in writing offended religious feelings, and was punishable by a fine of up to 3,800 Euros or three months imprisonment. In Israel, injury to religious sentiment is punishable by one year of imprisonment. Article 173 states that an offense of blasphemy occurs when "One publishes a publication that is liable to crudely offend the religious faith or sentiment of others." A word or even a sound heard in public that offends is punishable. Blasphemy is punishable by death in Islamic countries such as Afghanistan, Bangladesh, Pakistan, Saudi Arabia, and others

A human-like god is an artistic product of immature adult thinking. It is a greater blasphemy by far to ignore truth and to fail to comprehend that in adult thinking, a human-like god is a continuation of a childhood imaginary companion, and is artistically enhanced by adult use of abstract words.

The old adage is true, "I know that I am god, as when I pray I find I am talking to myself."

The cerebral cortex of the human brain is quite certainly the origin of an imagined human-like first father god. There is a god yet it is not outside of the brain but inside of it. The conscious human self needs a god but not the subconscious soul that silently evolves from an environment that is a continuation of a cosmological force.

The average person also hopes they do have a soul that survives physical death yet has little or no knowledge of how this can be so. What some refer to as a divinity inside of humans is the triune soul. A theistic religion represents the cerebral cortex of reason that projects an imaginary reasoning god, so as to direct the triune soul that forces life to live and by so doing to redirect humans to what is higher.

Humans are often helpless and frequently miserable, and this is why a human-like helper god is so important. Just a single incident during a happy day easily derails life for the worse and happiness often makes a swift departure. An invisible god assists humans to survive life and death.

Soulless

For the Middle East religions of Judaism, Christianity, and Islam, the physical body will be resurrected by a human-like first father god. A god is a bigger than life human-like ego that can resurrect and save the body from oblivion.

The religion of Judaism is soulless, inasmuch as only the living body is the real essence, and it is expected that a human-like god will resurrect it. Only a human-like god can restore life. No soul animates the body and only the ego of a human-like god can animate it. This is a great sin of separation, a sinful disconnect from the animating environment and the cosmos.

The Catholic Encyclopedia says of the soul, "Even uncivilized peoples arrive at the concept of the soul almost without reflection, certainly without any severe mental effort." Based upon this amusing statement, the very religion that Christianity is a continuation of is an even less than primitive and unreflective fixation on the physical body and its resurrection. Why did not the god of the Jews endow them with a soul? The Jews have no concept of the animating soul and instead rely exclusively on their human-like first father god to resurrect the physical body. To explain the beginning of life, the Jews did not focus on the earth and what animated life inside, instead they fixated on an imaginary companion, a human-like genealogical first father god. A glorified human-like god reflects only the glorious egocentric interest of humans.

This uncivilized ideology has no place in a civilized modern scientific society. The time will arrive when these wrongly conceived views of a human-like first father god and a resurrection of the physical body will be rightly seen for what they are, egocentric and barbaric notions. Yet since a majority of humankind accept these erroneous theistic views, they will fade slowly but fade away they will.

The god did not make the environment with his hands but with his ideas and mouth. The god had the idea to make the first human, not by a sexual act but formed the man from the earth and the woman from the man. However, humans were made flawed and soon became willfully disobedient. In reality, it is the idea of a human-like god that is flawed. The idea of a human-like god is a flawed making by the cerebral cortex of the human brain that fashions a genealogical beginning into a human-like first father god.

The intelligence of the male god fantastically formed his first offspring from the passive body of the earth which is not an equal to the human-like male god. As conceived in the cerebral cortex of the Jewish brain, life began from the real earth but was fashioned by an unreal imaginary companion of a human-like god. Since the god made the great earth, the male god is greater. The earth is made mildly human-like and feminized to open "her mouth" (Genesis 4:11) but cannot think.

The earth is secondary to the human-like male god and so humans must unkindly "subdue" (Genesis 1:28) it as ordered. To subdue means to "bring under control by physical force, to establish ascendency over, to overpower and conquer, and to cultivate land." Theists prefer to see a human-like god as the primary origin of life and the earth as secondary. In reality the origin of life is a continuation of the earth environment.

Resurrection

The Nicene and Apostles Creeds of the Christian Catholic and Protestant churches both conclude with the statement of faith of looking forward in time to the resurrection of the body of those dead and of a future physical life existence. Various polls on religion generally show that the American population is on average seventy-five to eighty percent Christian, and that approximately ninety percent of Americans accept the view there is a human-like god. For Christians, a range of polls show from sixty to ninety percent of them accept the physical resurrection of Jesus. The majority do not see Jesus as rising from the dead on his own but that it was an act performed by a human-like god.

The convoluted view of the body and soul by the Christian religion reveals an inept and confusing theology. Many early Christians were Jews and undoubtedly favored the resurrection of the body over the Greek and Roman view of a soul that survived death and journeyed to an afterlife under the earth in Hades. The gospels emphasize the physical resurrection of Jesus, and that his body survived death, not his ghost, spirit, or pneuma. (Luke 24:39; John 20:27)

Therefore, modern Christian denominations such as Jehovah's Witnesses, Seventh Day Adventists, Church of God, Amish and Mennonites have the view there is no soul and that the physical remains of the person rests until resurrection of the body. This includes both resurrection of the just and unjust on a last or final day of judgement.

In vivid contrast, mainstream Protestant religions are influenced more by Greek thinking of a psyche or soul that transits directly after death to an afterlife dimension.

The Baptist view is that humans do have a soul that is judged immediately after death, with the good person entering heaven and the evil person enters hell to be punished. There is no waiting for the last or final judgement. They take as support for this view the gospel words of the Greek physician Luke. Being Greek, Luke was writing for Greeks who were of course familiar with the view of a psyche or soul leaving the body at the time of death.

"And Jesus said unto him, Verily I say unto thee, Today shalt thou be with me in paradise." (Luke 23:43)

The view that humans have a soul and go directly to the afterlife of a heaven or hell is also accepted by Methodist and Presbyterian churches. Deceased individuals wait in the afterlife for the final judgement and resurrection and the rejoining of the soul with the physical body. Catholics also accept this view and add another dimension between heaven and hell known as purgatory. This is an intermediate state where sins are purged so the person can eventually proceed to heaven. This view is nonbiblical.

The United Methodist Church allows for cremation and organ donation of the body. Methodists accept the resurrection of the physical body of Jesus after his death yet for Christian followers there will instead be a pneuma or an ethereal or breath-like spiritual body resurrection as mentioned by the evangelist Saul or Paul. (I Corinthians 15:42-44)

Greek Savior

Was Jesus a Greek? While it seems evident that Jesus was not born into or a member of the Greek culture, nevertheless his thinking and words seem to be much influenced by it.

For Judaism and those Christian religions lacking the concept of a soul, then the physical body and the saving of it by a human-like god is necessary and mandatory. The resurrection of the body was necessary for Jews during the time of Jesus and continues to this day.

For those Christians following this way of thinking, the soul of Jesus did not go to heaven but his nephesh, his resurrected living breathing physical body made the journey.

In contrast, the Greeks spoke of the psyche or soul that survived physical death. Jesus was very likely influenced by Greek thinking on the psyche or soul. Yet in general, the psyche traveled to an afterlife underground of Hades. Jesus accepted the immortal psyche or soul and probably glimpsed a transition not to an underground Hades but to an ethereal afterlife dimension. This became his good news that he learned from the Greek culture. However, this insight was plastered over with the Jewish resurrection myth of the body that was added to the gospels and discussed in the epistles. The words of Jesus suggest he saw himself and others as having an animating soul.

"And when he was demanded of the Pharisees, when the kingdom of God should come, he answered them and said, The kingdom of God cometh not with observation: Neither shall they say, Lo here!, lo there! For behold, the kingdom of God is within you." (Luke 17: 20-21)

Obviously by this remark, the kingdom of the god is not the afterlife nor the life to come in the future. There is no actual personality of a god within a person, as it would then be feasible to make a diagnosis of a multiple personality disorder.

The statement also contains an unintended meaning of truth, and that is the imaginary companion of a human-like first father god is located only inside the human brain. The statement may also unintentionally refer to the cerebral cortex of the brain that is capable of a better or higher godly attitude of love and forgiveness so as to lessen conflict among humans.

What Jesus is most likely referring to in this verse from the gospel of Luke, is that the true ruling animating force that makes life to grow and go, is the soul. This is a plain influence of Greek thinking.

No other Israelite or Jew has or would so boldly declare that the place of a god or extra-physical ruling force is within humans. The soul is that which makes life to grow and to function, and that forces life to live and survive. Jesus points out it is difficult to observe the dwelling place of the god within. Jesus does not specifically say the psyche or soul is inside of humans but that an extra-natural something he refers to as a god is within that animates humans.

The statement by Jesus begs a question. Where is the place of a god, meaning a force inside of humans? Is it the blood or breathing, the brain or mind? The answer is that the ruling force is the triune soul that pervades the cells of the body and forces life to live as the hunger for food, sex and reproduction, and aggression.

Jesus also did not mention and by so doing, rejected the Jewish afterlife of Sheol. Jesus, the gospel authors, or translators of the New Testament did mention the Greek afterlife of Hades four times. For Jesus the afterlife is a dimension of a heaven, a place of ease for the good and the primitive concept and metaphor of a place of unease or dis-ease of the fire of Gehenna for the evil. Jesus also distorted his teachings by his continued cultural and metaphorical use of a human-like god, his affectionate abba or first father.

Growing up in the town of Nazareth in northern Israel, Jesus lived less than four miles or an hour walk from the Greco-Roman town of Sepphoris, the mountain capital town of the province of Galilee. The town had a large paved colonnaded street, an amphitheater, and many fine Roman buildings containing mosaics. Surely Jesus and his father Joseph worked in the town during a renovation project that occurred there during his youth. Jesus must also have watched the plays performed in the amphitheater. Evidence for this assertion is that he used the Greek work hypokrities, meaning actor, eighteen times in the gospels. The English word is hypocrite.

As regards the soul, Jesus was Greek in his thinking. His very name he is known by today is Greek rather than him being known by his Aramaic name Yashua. The fisherman disciple Shimon or Simeon bar Yona (died circa 64 CE) was even renamed and given the name Peter, in Greek petros, meaning rock. Jesus says in words attributed to him:

"And I say also unto thee, That thou art Peter, and upon this rock I will build my church...." (Matthew 16:18)

For the Greeks the body was not able to be saved but the essence of the body, the psyche or soul continued to exist. The Greek Christian theologian Origen Adamantius (185-254 CE), was an early church father who lived in Alexandria Egypt. He was schooled in Greek philosophy including Plato and Aristotle, and in Christian writings. It was Origen who wrote on the immortal soul and influenced the later Roman Catholic teaching of a soul. Origen writes:

"It can be shown that an incorporeal and reasonable being has life in itself independently of the body...then it is beyond a doubt bodies are only of secondary importance and arise from time to time to meet the varying conditions of reasonable creatures. Those who require bodies are clothed with them and contrariwise, when fallen souls have lifted themselves up to better things their bodies are once more annihilated. They are ever vanishing and ever reappearing."

The words written by Origen show why he was not considered for sainthood by the early Catholic church. For Origen, there is something that animates life independent of the body, and this argues against a bodily resurrection dependent on a human-like god. Origen states that souls lift themselves up, suggesting a human-like god is not involved. Souls and bodies are ever vanishing and reappearing without a need for a human-like god to overtly intervene in this numinous activity. Origen was on the right track away from puerile dependence on a patriarchal human-like god, yet he was inevitably enmeshed in the mire of anthropomorphism from which he could not extricate himself. Having courage, he was on the right track by emphasizing the soul. He persisted and worked around "the elephant in the room," the imagined, obtruding, and ballooned conception of a human-like god in his brain.

Even the gospels are somewhat reminiscent of a Greek tragedy play. Yet instead of theater, the life drama of Jesus is talked about in sermons and read to the under educated during religious services.

The gospel of Luke and the Book of Acts, was intended by its author for an educated Greek audience. The author of the gospel of John wrote while living in the Greek colony of Ephesus, today located on the Mediterranean coast of Turkey. The earliest extant gospels of Mark, Matthew, Luke, John, the Epistles, and Book of Revelation are not written in Hebrew or Aramaic but in the Greek language.

Jesus Message

Little noticed and not commented on, some of the sayings of Jesus correct the grievous error of the Genesis Garden of Eden story. The error is with the story teller who portrays the human-like god to curse the first two humans for acquiring the knowledge of sex and reproduction, the harmful aggression displayed by Cain to his brother Abel, and the curse of having to till the soil and herd animals so as to obtain daily food. In the Garden the first two humans are portrayed as acquiring bad or evil knowledge. However, the really bad knowledge is that of the story teller who portrays the beginning of existence as a good human-like god who interacted with his knowledge acquiring good and evil offspring.

In the Genesis story, the human-like god is the goodness that begins the goodness of the environment and life. The human story teller deposits goodness in a single spot, the beginning. Yet goodness is not dispensed by nor is goodness a real attribute of a human-like god. A human-like god is only a symbol, a human way of identifying the unknown mechanism of a beginning of the environment and life.

As advocated by his human followers and representatives, the human-like god of the Jews is located exclusively outside of humans. In contrast, while accepting the metaphor of human-like, for Jesus the place of god is also inside of humans and living forms. This is his repairing of the separating sin of Judaism, of having only a life and not a soul. For Jesus the god becomes a metaphorical loving first father who made a special afterlife as a refuge from life for the surviving soul.

"And when he was demanded of the Pharisees, when the kingdom of God should come, he answered them and said, The kingdom of God cometh not with observation: Neither shall they say, Lo here!, lo there! For behold, the kingdom of God is within you." (Luke 17:20-21)

In the verses that follow Luke 17:20-21, there is no real discussion of the meaning of these particular verses. The verses convey the meaning that the animating force is also inside as an immanent soul. In a sense, the words of Jesus partially correct the sin of separation that occurred in the Garden of Eden story. No longer was the presence of the god or animating force outside but is inside of humans and life as well. Jesus corrected the original sin, the separation of what is inside of humans with the outside. The inside of humans is considered by Jews to be just dirt or flesh formed from soil that after death can only be reanimated by a human-like god. Jesus pointed out the place where the god resides is also inside. The Israelite Jesus corrected the original Jewish sin of the ashes to ashes, dust to dust of the body, and the shade or shadow journeying to Sheol under the earth. Jews later added a physical resurrection that is totally dependent on being performed by a human-like god. For Jesus this sinful way of thinking is corrected by having the animating presence inside as a soul.

"And he said, So is the kingdom of God, as if a man should cast seed into the ground; And should sleep, and rise night and day, and the seed should spring and grow up, he knoweth not how." (Mark 4: 26-27)

What Jesus alludes to by his words, is that the unknown inside force that causes seeds to sprout and to grow, is the kingdom or place of a ruling force, immanent as that which grows living things. By another remark Jesus strongly suggests there is a vital force but no human-like god or an afterlife dimension within a loaf of bread. There is an unseen immanent force that leavens, expands, enlarges, and grows the leavening of dough. He also uses this effective analogy with barley corn and mustard seeds.

"Another parable spake he unto them; The kingdom of heaven is like unto leaven, which a woman took, and hid in three measures of meal, till the whole was leavened." (Matthew 13:33)

"For the earth bringeth forth fruit of herself; first the blade, then the ear, after that the full corn in the ear. But when the fruit is brought forth, immediately he putteth in the sickle, because the harvest is come. And he said, Where unto shall we liken the kingdom of God? or with what comparison shall we compare it? It is like a grain of mustard seed, which, when it is sown in the earth, is less than all the seeds that be in the earth: But when it is sown, it groweth up, and becometh greater than all herbs, and shooteth out great branches; so that the fowls of the air may lodge under the shadow of it." (Mark 4:28-32)

Jesus removed the separating sin of human-kind by directing attention to an animating force inside of humans. However, being an Israelite peasant, he did not relinquish the long utilized human-like first father god metaphor to identify the origin of existence. To love a human-like first father god is better than to fear his aggression of curses that humans incurred in Genesis. Yet, the Old Testament cursing and blood thirsty god appears in the New Testament to demand the blood of Jesus. The corrective message of Jesus was turned into a bloody sacrificial redemption offered to the metaphorical human-like god.

The kingdom of god is a metaphor for both an afterlife dimension, and also an animating force inside of humans that survives physical death. The corrective message of Jesus in toto is that there is an animating soul, and after death there is another natural dimension to where it transitions. The father god metaphor used by Jesus is only a crude way to identify another dimension that is a natural continuation of the earthly dimension. The animating coherent soul makes a natural transition to an afterlife dimension at the time of death. In today's language, the body is composed of quantum particles, atoms and electrons, and gross cells and organs. The animating soul force as a continuation of a sole cosmological force evolves a coherency that continues to exist.

Family Guy

The first father god of Jesus existed only in his brain as a much older cultural metaphor that he was not able to easily discard. Using the metaphor of an abba or father to counteract the orthodox stern commandment giving god, Jesus removed religion from control of official priest/rabbis and made the theistic religion more family friendly. Christians later emphasized and added his mother and birth story to the mix, and behold, Christianity became an appealing family religion that continues to this day. The commandment "Thou shalt love thy neighbor as thyself," (Mark 12:31; Matthew 22:39) further expanded Christianity to be a social religion.

Sculpture

Catholic sculpture of Jesus on the cross portrays the suffering and betrayals of social life. These real conditions of life are not relieved by an imagined companion of a human-like first father god. The metaphor of a merciful first father fails to save Jesus and likewise for other humans. The figure of Jesus represents that each is saved from life not by a human-like god but by merciful death and entry into the reality of another dimension. Jesus is then a figure of help waiting in the afterlife dimension, to assist those who will sooner or later arrive there.

In contrast, Indian sculpture artists often portray the generally society avoiding, forest-dwelling Buddha sitting cross-legged, his right hand held and supported by the left hand. The figure looks serene, meditatively focusing attention and observing inner processes of brain and body functions. He appears peaceful and magnificently sublime, having accomplished a most difficult task, to accurately observe and know the conscious self and the subconscious soul.

Animating Essence

Walking into a theistic religious building is a poor and common ritual attempt to comprehend what animates human life. Monumental buildings dedicated to the animating essence of life, said to be a human-like god, is the worst kind of error.

A theistic religious building is ostensibly a place of communication with a human-like god, who it is expected may arrive to view and listen to those assembled there. In reality, the building represents the human body that houses the triune soul that animates life. The animating essence of life is a triune soul that forces life to live, and is a continuation of a cosmological force that animates and moves all things into, through and out of existence. The building also represents an afterlife dimension where the soul will journey following physical death.

Though the body perishes, the soul is conserved to continue. Research evidence of near-death experiences, verified and documented childhood reincarnation memories, and experimental testing of authentic mediums, suggest that the animating force of earthly life is capable of existing in another dimension. Yet, in efforts to convey this phenomenon, early humans utilized the metaphor of a human-like first father god as the mechanism for the animation of life and an afterlife.

The animating force of biological life is a continuation of and is supported by the environment, and yet is also extra-biological and extra-environmental. It is a triune soul that forces life to live and to struggle to survive. Animated life is a continuation of an animated ancestral environment of energy, and in turn is a continuation of an animating cosmological force. What animates life is not exclusively confined to it, or to the earth. Animation of life is not limited and confined to what is visible but has roots and extends from and to, the invisible. What animates life is not isolated from the greater reality of the universe but extends beyond seeming boundaries to the boundless.

The animating motion of the visible environment is energy and the animating of energy is a cosmological force that exists on its own. Life is a continuation of this process as a triune soul force of hunger for food, sex and reproduction, and aggression that forces life to live.

Humans en masse have always found it difficult to deal with the animating motion and change of the environment, and with what animates life within.

For the general population then, the animator of both is a human-like god. Most humans cannot readily comprehend nor accept that the origin of the environment and life is an unhuman cosmological force.

The animating force within life is degraded by biblical theists to be a curse by a human-like god. Animation is of two kinds, the motion of the environment and of life. The movement of life is a continuation of the movement of the environment. The search for an unseen yet vaguely sensed animating force of life has led theists ignorantly and arrogantly to what is without as a separate human-like animator, a god.

The male god is only a projected personality for the triune soul, as hunger for food, sex and reproduction, and aggression that forces life to live and survive. A human-like god is the attempt to ethicize existence by humanizing the animating essence. A human-like god is necessary for many as it provides courage and confidence to continue living. When humans worship a theistic human-like male god, they are in reality only worshipping their own genealogy on the male line.

The Chinese do not need a god as do the Middle East religions of Judaism, Christianity, and Islam. The Chinese, as do all peoples, have superstitious folk religions of good and evil spirits. The Chinese also practice a form of ancestor remembrance and reverence, progressing back in time to various legendary emperor rulers. However, the Jews in pondering their origin, traced their lineage genealogically through the male line (Genesis 5) to Adam and then hypostatized and glorified a human-like first father god. Many, if not all, religions revere ancestors but Jews, Christians, and Muslims elevate the practice to a delusional level of a human-like first father god who will bring humans back to life through the resurrection of the physical body.

Rather than a god giving commandments, Confucius (551-479 BCE) studied prior teachings and gave teachings of his own on family values and social ethics. The religion of Taoism has no god but instead senses the elements of energy or chi in the environment. What refreshing mental hygiene.

Saved By the Soul

The animating soul is difficult to perceive and to correctly conceive, and there is much superstition about it. The problem for humans, is not a human-like god or a devil but the subconscious soul of life. It is the soul that is both the scourge and the savior of life. As a continuation of a cosmological force, and a continuation of the environment, the subconscious cauldron of the soul as hunger for food, sex and reproduction, and aggression, bubbles up into the faint realms of reasoning.

The human conscious cerebral cortex attempts to improve and direct the subconscious soul of the body and brain through reasoning. Yet reasoning also generates a false concept by measuring its way back in time to the beginning of humans and conceiving of it to be a human-like first father god. Evolved conscious reason seeks to find its way out of the subconscious body and brain by manufacturing a human-like god.

The oldest extant version of the earliest gospel of Mark, the Sinaiticus Codex (circa 330-360 CE), contains no body resurrection of Jesus, which was only later added, probably by circa 450 CE. In reality, the soul of Jesus as do all souls enter immediately into an afterlife dimension though a cosmological default of the conservation of energy.

Judaism and Israelite religion utilizes a human-like first father god to be the maker of physical humans. In this distortion of thinking the physical body must then be saved and restored by the maker of humans. In mainstream Christianity, the Greek concept of a psyche or soul is accepted as real and must then be reunited to the resurrected body on earth by the human-like god.

In India the atma sanely unites not with a previous dead resurrected body but by the soul reincarnating on its own to another body. This occurs not under the direction of a human-like god but as a continuing behavior of the cosmos to do so.

Subconscious willing of the triune soul seeks to gratify the life of the body, while conscious reasoning of the cerebral cortex seeks to comprehend and direct the triune soul that forces life to live and to survive. The soul continues to exist until calmed by self conscious discipline.

The real problem of living is not solved by a humanlike god but by meditative observation and study of the phenomena of the behavior of life, the environment, and the cosmos as a whole. Most problems of conscious life comes from the subconscious triune soul that forces life to live by obtaining food, having sex and reproducing, and aggression. Each is saved by the soul and yet each must be saved from the subconscious soul by the conscious self.

Life is a maze of many directions and of consciously choosing which way to go. The direction leading to both self and soul comprehension is real and best. A human-like god only furnishes a vague and distant role model, a murky and muddled subjective unreal human attempt to vicariously supervise and direct to what is good. Yet, for many, a human-like god is the only way to go in the direction of what is good in life.

God and Soul

Religion is not an observation based science, nor is it a mathematics system of measuring. Religion is an art that only and merely presents the beginning and function of the environment and life through imagined and expressive ideas. These ideas are expressed in sculpture, painting, and the abstract portrait of words as contained in theistic scriptures.

Science is a focus of attention to trial and error learning by observing and measuring (math) in the making of utilitarian tools, weapons, and dwellings. In contrast, theistic religion is an imaginary artistic expression, a false conception of the origin of existence to be a genealogical human-like first father god. Observing, measuring, and fashioning real objects is the proper area of science. Artistic imagination is the only means to fashion a genealogical human-like first father god, and appealing to faith is a way of continuing the false concept and shared delusion.

A genealogical human-like first father version of existence must be comprehended to be based on the childhood developmental phenomenon of an imaginary companion that is continued by immature and under-educated adults. Only an immature person needs an imaginary companion and human-like first father god. Lacking individual strength and encountering the turmoil and suffering of life and eventual death, the desperate need for protection imagines and glorifies human origin to be a protective human-like god. From only the subjective idea of a supernatural male parent as the origin of life, strength is summoned and relief is found to live, age, and die.

A human-like god serves to distract from life to what is beyond it. Theists advocate that a god has shaped life on earth, therefore it is imagined that he can also reshape the life of the body in a future resurrection. This imaginary thinking distracts attention from real life experience of pain and for some brings subjective relief.

The solution for the many distractions of life, is acceptance of one big imaginary distraction; a genealogical human-like first father god. This distraction from life is also supplemented with a series of smaller distractions and behaviors that bring temporary pleasures and satisfaction, such as: food, sex, aggression, drugs, career, possessions, and hobbies. The subjective pleasurable idea of a human-like god uplifts and transports many humans from dissatisfaction to an imagined satisfying reliever of the suffering of life.

In reality, life does not come from a subjective and imaginatively known human-like first father god but from the energy of the real objective supportive earth and an unknown cosmological force. As a continuation of a cosmological force, the soul of life has evolved from the earth. The growth of life is a continuation of both; a supportive outside environment, and inside the living body as a subconscious triune soul of hunger for food, sex and reproduction, and aggression that forces life to live.

The popular view of a religious celibate person is that since they can control themselves sexually, they are closer to a god or are more god-like. Celibacy is equated with a monotheistic god that does not indulge in physical sex, does not lust for food, and instead of aggression is mostly loving and rewarding, yet also punishes. The real meaning of the practice of celibacy and moderating food and aggression, is that the person has transcended the subconscious soul of life through self-conscious observation and by a balance of lifestyle.

Then instead of fawning over and obtaining approval and avoiding punishment by a human-like god, the subconscious soul is made fit by the guiding conscious self to remain in an afterlife dimension and not to return. Only the conscious self can save human life from the subconscious triune soul, never an imaginary and unreal human-like god.

Three Efforts

The three main efforts of life are for food, sex and reproduction, and aggression. Human effort is both subconscious and conscious but subconscious is primary. The subconscious efforts of the body are reflected in conscious sensations, brain images, and willing efforts. The conscious self can observe the subconscious soul that forces life to live.

The muscles of the body move to obtain food, and the smooth muscles of the intestinal tract move and break it down to nourish the cells and organs. The smooth muscles of the penis and clitoris move to swell and stiffen, and muscles of the body embrace and engage in intercourse. The muscles of the body work to compete and to survive economically and physically.

Individual subconscious and conscious effort to exist and to live is a continuation of cosmological effort and environmental motion. There is a continuous untiring effort to move the universe by a cosmological force that ever exists on its own. There is an effort in quantum particles, atoms, and electrons to exist and to move. Life is a subconscious and conscious continuation of this non-conscious procession of effort.

Death

Few there are who know how to live, and even fewer know how to die. It is not always possible to be certain about what will happen next in life, therefore for most it is quite uncertain what will occur after death. However, both Buddhism and Christianity do have ways of making an individual aware and accepting of the eventual experience of death.

Buddhist meditation includes meditating on death by visualizing the body and its differing parts, swollen, turned black and blue, festering, rotting, smelling and stinking, consumed by maggots, eaten by animals, bones scattered, bleached white by the sun, reduced to powder, and blown away by the wind. Buddhists also meditate on letting go of possessiveness and sadness, they practice living in the world and clinging to naught, accepting many inevitable experiences of life, ageing, and death.

The Christian ghastly portrayal of Jesus on the cross is both the worship of goodness, love, compassion, and an anticipation of suffering that leads to death. The contemplation of the artwork also contributes to acceptance of the inevitable sequence of suffering that will surely occur during life. Identifying with the suffering of Jesus is a way to get through and past the tribulations of earthly life to another and better dimension.

The comedian George Carlin (1937-2008) joked, "Dying must have survival value. Or it wouldn't be part of the biological process." (2001, Napalm & Silly Putty) The philosopher Arthur Schopenhauer (1788-1860) makes a similar statement.

"For us death is and remains something negative, the cessation of life; but it must also have a positive side that nevertheless remains hidden from us because our intellect is quite incapable of grasping it. We therefore know quite well what we lose, but not what we gain through death." (Parega and Paralipomena, Vol. 2)

The positive side of death is twofold; it is either a transition to oblivion or to another dimension. The gain of death at a minimum is that it removes biological and emotional suffering. Death also usefully serves to show the futility of frivolous life efforts and endeavors, and therefore can contribute to moderating life and to acceptance of an inevitable and eventual demise.

A calm peaceful death of old age is a euthanasia, a good death that removes each individual from the burdens, struggles, and pains of life. Some struggle toward the good rest of biological death. Most struggle through life toward the hoped for and believed reward of another dimension that extends beyond the earthly one. An individual can be convinced by the accumulated evidence for either the continuation of life in a dimension that differs from the earth, or a merciful natural oblivion from the toil and turmoil of life. Either potential outcome is good.

Supportive Evidence

Over time the pleasure of eating food wanes, and sex and aggression become less forceful. The triune soul force lessens its presence in the biology of the body. Cells and organs through injury and ageing develop irreparable damage and disrepair. Though the soul is willing, the flesh is weak. As a continuation of cosmological force, human willing for food, sex, and aggression, continues to exist after physical death. Like a record or compact disc, grooved subconscious habits form. The triune soul force as a kind of imprint or afterimage, disengages from the body. The reality of another dimension where the soul that forces life to live, departs to after physical death is supported by:

Anecdotal experience.
Childhood phenomenon of an imaginary companion.
Near-death experience.
Authentic mediumship.
Verified and documented childhood reincarnation memories.

Anecdotal experience of an afterlife dimension has been revealed in innumerable personal stories, surveys, and case studies.

Individuals through the years have communicated stories to other family members and friends about seeing, hearing, or feeling the presence of deceased persons as spirits or ghosts while waking or seeing them during dreams.

Studies suggest that perhaps as many as seventy percent of children have an imaginary friend or companion that they interact with during play. It is possible that all children have an innate tendency to engage in play with an imaginary companion. A child's imaginary companion can be a child, adult, animal, or a ghost of a deceased family member or person. A child may spontaneously speak of an imaginary companion usually in the age range of from two through nine years. This innate developmental cognitive process fades during maturation.

A child spontaneously imagines a companion as a way of playing, exploring, learning, and practicing relationship interaction. An imaginary companion is not the result of a failure to socialize or a psychological disorder. Having an imaginary companion or friend is a way for a child to practice communication when friends or family are not readily available. A percentage of imaginary companions may also be deceased family members or unknown persons. In some case studies, children do obtain accurate information from their imaginary companions, such as names, how they died, locations, and dates of certain events.

The International Association for Near-Death Studies is an organization formed in the United States in 1981 for the purpose of studying and disseminating knowledge of the phenomenon of near-death experience. Reports of an afterlife dimension may occur after an experience of being pronounced clinically dead. Reports may include a sense of being out of the body, movement through some kind of tunnel or enclosure, encountering deceased relatives and friends, encountering religious or spiritual figures and a bright light, having a life review, and a resuscitated return to the body. Science is bringing its methods of close observation to bear on what happens after death and what those who have near-death experiences claim about the existence of an afterlife dimension.

A medium is a person who can see, hear, and feel those who are deceased. Most humans focus only on surface appearance of forms, and are blind to the dimension of energy/force of which they are composed. Mediums focus attention on both visible and nonvisible energy.

Modern mediums such as John Edward (1969-present), Teresa Caputo (1966-present), George Anderson (19??-present), and other reputable individuals, have provided many hours of public and private evidential results for those interested. The readings of authentic mediums do bring through some eye-opening details. Even if not sure proof of survival and an afterlife dimension, information obtained during a reading by an authentic medium can be thought provoking and meaningful, even to a sceptic.

During his career, psychiatrist Ian Stevenson (1918-2007) investigated over twenty-five hundred childhood cases of reincarnation covering a span of forty years. He was funded by the inventor of the photocopy Xerox machine, Chester Carlson (1906-1968) who was interested in reincarnation. Carlson left one million dollars in his will to endow a department chair at the University of Virginia, and he bequeathed an additional one million dollars to Dr. Stevenson personally to enable him to continue his research into cases of childhood reincarnation.

During his meticulous research, Stevenson found that young children often recall memories of past lives when between two and five years of age. Stevenson and his assistants found reporting of past life memories by children to be more reliable and verifiable than are adult reports.

Reincarnation

Reincarnation is the view that "an individual dies yet survives physical death to be born again in another body." This definition suggests that the soul of a person survives in a coherent way and resides in another dimension prior to entering a new body at some time during conception and birth.

There are various common terms for the reincarnation process. These include palingenesis, (Greek palin, again, and genesis, birth); metempsychosis (Greek meta, beyond, and empsukhos, animate); transmigration, (Latin, transmigrare, to move from place to place; and samsara (Sanskrit, continuous movement) the round or cycle of birth, death, and rebirth.

Reincarnation is a widespread majority view that approximately sixty percent of the earth's population accept as true, while the remaining minority of forty percent accept the view of having only one lifetime. Acceptance of reincarnation in the United States hovers around an average of twenty-five to thirty percent. Historically, the Norse and Celts accepted reincarnation, and today most of India and Asia continue to accept reincarnation, as well as Australian Aborigines, North and South American Indian tribes, Eskimos, Druze peoples in the Middle East, and Hasidim Jews. An interesting distinction between Hindu views of reincarnation and that of Native Americans, is that in India rebirth is viewed as a process to be avoided. Native Americans generally look forward to returning to an earthly life.

The view of reincarnation advocates that like air, food, and water, that go into and out of the body again, so too can a subtle soul force enter, leave, and enter human body cells again. Many unknown and also well-known western individuals have accepted and advocated the view of reincarnation, and some insist they were reincarnated. Just a few of these notable personages include:

Socrates (469-399 BCE)
Rumi (1207-1273)
Napoleon (1769-1821)
Arthur Schopenhauer (1788-1860)
Ralph Waldo Emerson (1803-1882)
Benjamin Franklin (1706-1790)
Henry David Thoreau (1817-1862)
Walt Whitman (1819-1892)
Paul Gauguin 1848-1903)
Mark Twain (1835-1910)
Jack London (1876-1916)
George Patton (1885-1945)

Henry Ford (1863-1947)
George Harrison (1943-2001)
Ian Stevenson (1918-2007)

These distinguished individuals were intelligent, much more so than the average person and follower of theism. At least some small credence should be given to their personal experience and acceptance of reincarnation.

Unsaved

Through consistent meditation practice, attentive observation develops focus and ceases to be distracted by changing sensations of seeing, hearing, smelling, tasting, and touching. Attention becomes calmed and can better examine brain images, observed to have a beginning and ending and are fleeting. Attention may then be drawn to body and brain, and to that which forces life to live, a forcible hunger for food, forcible drive for sex and reproduction, and forcible aggression of emotions and behaviors. This innate force is the triune soul as a forcible continuation of the energy elements of the earth that broods all of life. The environment is a direct and forcible continuation of what moves the universe, an unseen non-phenomenal numinous and sole cosmological force that ever exists on its own.

Conscious sensations continually change from second to second. Brain images of now, past, and future are fleeting. With practice, conscious attention eventually comes to observe the subconscious background of a triune soul force as a forcible hunger for food, sex and reproduction, and aggression. Then is clearly observed that the soul force of living takes place dependent on the background of the local environment. Also observed is that the earth environment occurs dependent upon the background of the sun, moon, and stars that are all moved by a sole cosmological force that ever exists.

Meditative attention is salvational as it reduces and disengages the triune soul force from its forcing of individual life to live and the consequent retaining of subconscious habits and space-time images. Meditative observation dissipates the triune soul that forces life to live by tracing it to its forcible origin, and by reducing its content of habits and image stores; and by so doing becomes unsaved.

Developing an unsaved dynamic, an individual is saved from the ever recurring round of time and dimensional existence.

Brief History of Spiritualism

One of the few indigenous American religions, Spiritualism claims to reveal an afterlife dimension but like any other group, authenticity, ignorance, and deception exists. In Spiritualism, individuals known as "mediums" claim to see a dimension where souls continue to exist.

During the twentieth century some of these claims have been tested and found to be authentic, while other claimants only pretend to see, are deceptive and fraudulent. Spiritualism is an American religion having perhaps five to ten thousand members in the United States and small numbers in other countries. What contributes to keeping the religion's followers small in number is:

1. It is considered evil by leaders and members of theistic and predominant Catholic and Protestant religions.
2. As in any other field of endeavor there are frauds.
3. There are only a small minority of individuals who have authentic ability to communicate with the deceased.
4. The religion teaches reliance on cause and effect.
5. Few comprehend the importance of its teachings.

The American religion of Spiritualism began in the year 1848 in a small town of that time known as Hydesville in upstate New York. On or about the evening of March 31, 1848, the two younger Fox sisters, Kate 11 and Margaret age 14 convinced their older sister Leah and parents, they were interacting with the ghost of a deceased peddler.

What was even more spectacular was that the peddler communicated with the sisters through rapping noises that all who came to observe the phenomenon, plainly heard and recorded the events in written testimony. Word spread of the communication with spirits. Soon the two Fox sisters were demonstrating communication with spirits publically and in private sessions and enjoyed success as mediums. Both sisters were considered to be talented mediums, able to produce spirit raps, spirit lights, spirit writing, and ghostly appearing materialized hands. However, during success over the years, both sisters began to drink wine and consequently developed behaviors of alcohol abuse and alcoholism.

Eventually Margaret confessed that the rapping sounds had been a hoax and explained how as young girls, herself and her sister Kate had tied an apple to a string and bumped it or dropped it to roll on the floor. Margaret claimed she and her sister had deceived the parents and neighbors into the view that a ghost was haunting the house.

On October 21, 1888, at the New York Academy of Music, with Margaret on stage and Kate in the audience, the sisters were paid fifteen hundred dollars (a large sum of money in those days) by a newspaper reporter to demonstrate how the rapping sounds evident at séances were produced. In front of an audience of two-thousand people Margaret demonstrated raps heard by all in the theater. Doctors came on stage to verify that the raps were produced by manipulating an ankle joint in her feet. Margaret also later signed a confession which was published in the New York World newspaper of the time. Margaret made very strong statements in publications against Spiritualism, as she stated:

"That I have been chiefly instrumental in perpetrating the fraud of Spiritualism upon a too-confiding public, most of you doubtless know. The greatest sorrow in my life has been that this is true, and though it has come late in my day, I am now prepared to tell the truth, the whole truth, and nothing but the truth, so help me God!...I am here tonight as one of the founders of Spiritualism to denounce it as an absolute falsehood from beginning to end, as the flimsiest of superstitions, the most wicked blasphemy known to the world."

Strong words of condemnation but just over one year later after her foot joint-cracking exhibition, Margaret recanted her confession in writing in November, 1889. A copy of this recantation appears in Marilyn J. Autry's book, *Light From Beyond the Tomb*, (pp. 56-68). In the document Margaret states that her sister Kate was also in complete agreement with her recantation. "She is in complete sympathy with me. She did not approve of my past course."

Margaret refers to those who influenced her to denounce Spiritualism with the words:

"...the treacherous horde who held out promises of wealth and happiness in return for an attack on Spiritualism, and whose helpful assurances were so deceitful... At the time I was in great need of money and persons who I prefer for the present not to name, took advantage of the situation...." She stated that her previous critical statements against Spiritualism "...were false in every particular."

Relevant to both of her statements is that previously in 1852, Margaret met a physician and adventurous explorer by the name of Elisha Kent Kane and married him in 1856. During their acquaintance and marriage, Kane who was Roman Catholic, thought Margaret and her sister Kate were frauds as was the religion of Spiritualism. He urged her on many occasions to refrain from the practice of Spiritualism. By May of 1853 Margaret had given her promise to Kane she would not practice Spiritualism any longer. Prior to this promise, Margaret's last séance was for President Franklin Pierce's wife Jane whose young son had died in a train accident.

In 1856 Kane married Margaret in a private ceremony and the couple was to have a public declaration when he returned from a trip. However Kane died in 1857 and Margaret dropped out of sight for over a year as she was ill and depressed over his untimely death. Perhaps to honor her deceased beloved, in August of 1858 Margaret became a member of the Roman Catholic Church and was baptized at St. Peter's church in New York City. However, as time went by, Margaret resumed her practice as a medium in the religion of Spiritualism.

Further in the record of her 1889 recantation, Margaret reveals who influenced her to denounce Spiritualism as a fraud. It was she said:

"...persons high in the Catholic church..." and in a letter received from a "Cardinal Manning" she states he urged her to "...abandon this wicked work of the devil." Speaking of the Catholic Church Margaret states, "You know it hates everything opposed to its tenets, and will not spare any means to blot from existence any persons or sect that does not agree with its doctrines. Selfishness and hatred, I suppose, were the motives by which those Catholics were actuated…this effort was made by a powerful society of that persuasion in London."

Controversial to the end, Kate (July 2, 1892) and Margaret (March 8, 1893) died in poverty and the remains of both were eventually interred in the same grave in Cypress Hill Cemetery in Brooklyn, New York. For the sisters at least, the controversy of their lives was over.

Overview of Spiritualism

The self-reliant American attitude of the religion that came to be known as Spiritualism, claims to peek directly into the afterlife dimension. During the 1800s it spread rapidly to an estimated nine million members in the United States. The religion of Spiritualism spread rapidly as it undoubtedly contained some appealing or even great truths. However, for modern critics this statement of "great" and "truth" about such a minor religion seems to be an oxymoron like jumbo shrimp, or military intelligence. It cannot be denied that the Fox sisters experienced a life of controversy, but what they and the religion of Spiritualism at least point to is not a fraud, and it is evident that the religion made some important accomplishments. The teachings of Spiritualism:

1. Partially removed anthropomorphism from the origin of existence.
2. Promoted communication with the dimension or dimensions of afterlife existence.
3. Suggest that human evolution is extra dimensional.

The religion of Spiritualism says the origin of existence is not a personal god, it is an "Infinite Intelligence" which is a form of pantheism, the view that it is everywhere infinitely present. Infinite Intelligence is not a personality but is immanent in the finite functions and order of the environment and living forms. For Spiritualism there is no personal human-like god.

Yet members of the religion could not bring themselves to completely drop the human-like god of western religion, and refer to the origin of existence as Infinite Intelligence, and so it continues to be human-like.

Spiritualist teachings emphasize following the Infinite Intelligence expressed in "nature's physical and spiritual laws." Yet an Infinite Intelligence is an influence of theistic religion and its assumptions, and it is well known what happens when someone assumes. The view that the origin of existence has an intelligence is anthropomorphism, the use of human attributes. The term Infinite Intelligence is a cognitive reluctance to relinquish the anthropomorphism of a disembodied human-like god.

Like the view of a theistic god, when the concept of pantheism in Spiritualism is looked at closely, the view is not supported by credible evidence. Any sane person would have to question the reality of such an immanent intelligence as the plain evidence is that existence contains many mistakes and evils. Can a good Infinite Intelligence make finite mistakes and exist in what is evil? What kind of Infinite Intelligence would make mistakes such as genetic mutations, birth defects, disease and parasites, and exist as harmful environmental destruction such as earthquakes and hurricanes? Where is Infinite Intelligence in the suffering of animals consuming each other while still alive, and the capacity for human evil and brutal aggression and sufferings of crime and war?

A god is a human way of measuring an unmeasurable cosmological force that is also immanent in all. There is a causal order to existence but there is no intelligence. There is an unknowing cosmological force that moves a natural cause and effect order of change, as all relative forces of gravity and electromagnetism, energy of elements, the material mass of environmental forms, and living forms.

The cosmological force that moves existence does so from all sides, everywhere, from outside and inside. There is an order to existence such as random wave action of water and winds on the beach that distribute patterns of sand and shells. To say the origin of existence has intelligence is based only on the coherent order and cause-effect sequence of events.

Cause and effect change is not a human-like intelligence; it only orders things to function as a variable progression in time. A cosmological origin of existence is a power or greater force but has no theological intelligence or judgment.

What unfolds and grows a fertilized egg cell? While there is observed a cause and effect order, it cannot be said there is a pantheistic intelligence within as the genes and chromosomes often mutate and malfunction to cause many types of harmful birth defects, medical disorders, and death. There is only an immanent force that moves the sperm to unite with the egg, and the cells to grow, that ignites the heart to beat, the brain to perceive and conceive, and the genitals to reproduce.

In reality, there are elements of energy inside environmental forms, and there is a triune soul inside living forms but not an intelligence. The triune soul of hunger for food, sex and reproduction, and aggression, is an innate force to survive. Hunger for food, sex and reproduction, and aggression, have sprung from and are a continuation of the environment that is a continuation of a cosmological force that moves the universe.

Human behavior has an origin in the behavior of the environment, not in the behavior of a human-like god. The biology of molecular life comes from the earth while the essence of life is a continuation of a cosmological force. The essence of life is a triune soul force of hunger for food, sex and reproduction, and aggression that forces life to live as a continuation of a sole cosmological force. Life is dependent on the environment but as a continuation of a cosmological force transcends it.

There is an unknowing outside moving force that moves inside of all things. There is cause and effect order, coherence, and disorder but no intelligence. Spiritualism's concept of Infinite Intelligence is not personal and so cannot be appealed to for anything. It is a pantheistic presence inherent in the struggle and suffering life of good and evil experience.

The word religion is derived from the Latin prefix "re," meaning again, and the suffix "ligare," to connect. Spiritualists say they reconnect to an Infinite Intelligence that orders the behaviors of the physical and nonphysical environment. Yet the most important reconnecting practice of Spiritualism is contact with a usually unperceived dimension or dimensions of an afterlife existence where souls of the deceased continue to exist.

Those who come to Spiritualism, through their own experience or through experience with an evidential medium, come to recognize the truth of the dimensions of existence, and that the earth is but one dimension and an afterlife is another dimension. Awareness of an afterlife dimension does not in any way depend on and is not controlled by a human-like god who can prevent humans from having access to it.

The only true American religion is Spiritualism. The significance of early Spiritualism is that it directed attention to and stimulated interest in personal experience of another dimension of reality. The direct experiential contact with dimensions of the afterlife is what enthralled some people in upstate New York, in the years following March 31, 1848 with the founding of modern Spiritualism.

However, like any other endeavor, such as the fields of religion, law, medicine, finance, and sales, there are frauds that prey on the trusting. But this is not to say that the whole field of religion, law, medicine, finance, and sales are corrupt. While the Fox sisters and Spiritualism like any other human endeavor certainly inspired fraudulent practice, the importance of the sisters is that they also certainly inspired some people with genuine mediumistic abilities. The Fox sisters certainly inspired many to come forward and to share their ability with their fellow humans. The revealing of another dimension which could be experienced by those able to see, remains as a small historical brightness for humankind.

Like other religions, Spiritualism offers the comfort of an afterlife dimension but most importantly it also offers contact with the souls residing there. Spiritualism with its claims of perceiving an afterlife dimension, also points to a further path of evolution.

A cosmological force that moves as a continuation within life forms on earth is the same force that moves souls in other dimensions. Spiritualism is a version of evolution, an evolution of dimensions to compliment Charles Darwin's (1809-1882) physical earthly evolution. In fact both views began around the same time. Darwin had the idea of evolution in 1838 but did not publish until 1859, while modern Spiritualism began with the Fox sisters March 31, 1848.

There is scientific evidence for the evolution of energy as elements; there is much fossil evidence for physical evolution of plants, animals, and humans. There is convincing anecdotal evidence for continued afterlife evolution such as the near-death experience that often mentions reincarnation, childhood reports of reincarnation memories, and mediumistic evidential readings during which relatives and friends appear. Protestant Christianity influenced early Spiritualists to deny the view of reincarnation but today Spiritualism does not take a stand on the view, and instead leaves it up to individual conscience to accept or reject the view.

Middle East religions teach there is a greater human-like god, and teach humans to obey the first father. The Jews follow the commandment rules, Christians love their neighbors and love a greater first father god, and Muslims submit their individual will to a greater will of Allah. In Spiritualism, no god or devil can assist or resist humans, only former human souls can communicate, assist, inspire, and guide. The individual has to be responsible for his or her behaviors to an Infinite Intelligence, in reality cause and effect of movement and order.

In the religion of Spiritualism a god does not respond to humans but departed souls can and do. The cosmological force within all things as movement and causal order does not respond to humans, it only moves each through life to both good and the evil of harm.

Spiritualism has no human-like god and no devil. It does not need them as it relies on what the religion calls "Natural Law," a residue of anthropomorphism. In reality, there are no laws, as laws imply a lawmaker.

There are only natural behaviors of relative forces, energies, and forms of the stable environment. The behavior of living forms is a continuation of the behavior of the environment.

There are no laws in the universe, only repetitive behaviors of the environment and living forms. The real teacher of humans is the natural environment that gives life to, supports, and kills living forms. Imitating the behavior of the natural teacher, so do humans raise plants and animals, support and protect and harvest and kill them. Humans also give birth to their own and kill other humans.

For many this is why a greater authoritative and compassionate human-like presence is required. In the natural behavior of the environment, the origin of humans is imagined to be the behavior of a greater human-like first father god. The only recourse the human brain, specifically the cerebral cortex has is to imagine a human-like beginning as a way of obtaining protection from the environment and other life forms and fellow humans.

What Spiritualists are really relying on is not a law but cause and effect change and behavior, and it is this that both rewards and punishes. Spiritualism teaches that the natural laws governing existence are derived from an Infinite Intelligence existing both outside and inside of all things. In reality, the environment has no laws, which are a human concept. Nature or the environment has only behaviors that are observed to be repetitive and often reliable enough for human purposes of behavior.

Spiritualism teaches that by obeying or disobeying nature's cause and effect changes, a person either becomes happy or unhappy. But being unhappy is the rule of existence not the exception and unhappiness frequently follows the best of conscious intentions.

Henry David Thoreau (1817-1862) said, "Most men lead lives of quiet desperation and go to the grave with the song still in them." So not only do most live a life of desperation and never achieve peace in life, most take the desperation of life with them to the afterlife.

Humans are desperate about physical and emotional health, about relationships of love and sex, of spouse and children and friends, and desperate about money and a job. Most suffer silently, some seek solace by talking with relatives and friends, and some turn to professional advice of a doctor or psychologist. Some turn to a human-like god and pray and may obtain only some chance answer and direction. Spiritualists turn to the cause and effect environment, and turn to departed souls for answers, assistance, and to obtain direction. Yet there exists as much struggle, conflict, and suffering among Spiritualists as among individuals of any theistic religion, and agnostic or atheist group.

In theistic religions, a human-like god began existence, oversees life, and oversees an afterlife dimension. This hypostatization of a god was conflated with anecdotal experiences of dimensions of an afterlife. No evidence exists at all for a human-like god, only faith and belief support the view. Yet there is much anecdotal and also some scientific evidence for the existence of another dimension and an afterlife. The great truth of the small religion of Spiritualism is that there is another dimension sans a human-like god.

Those who come to Spiritualism in various ways recognize the truth of dimensions of existence. There is no need for a maker of these dimensions. All dimensions (a quality of spatial extension or a level of existence) that humans are aware of are natural, such as height, width, depth, and time, as well as dimensions of the environment of earth, water, air, light, energy, and life. The dimension of the afterlife is a natural continuum of all other dimensions.

A prominent medium in the religion of Spiritualism by the name of the Reverend Eloise Page (1910-2007) made the following statement, "We are a light on the path to those who find us." Side-stepping any who are unscrupulous, there is no doubt that humankind will in the future confirm the truth of these words made by a well-known contemporary of modern Spiritualism.

Touting

The religion of Spiritualism touts an Infinite Intelligence that all things come from and that indwells them. Spiritualists are comforted by the mere thought of a background Infinite Intelligence with no evidence for its objective existence. This dogma is based on mere speculation and/or the observed semi-order of the environment and life. No human-like god or any kind of intelligence crafted intelligent humans. Only the supportive environment, genetics, and trial and error learning has shaped the intelligence of species and individuals. Yet the religion of Spiritualism attracts many who look forward to basking in the presence of a higher intelligence as instant relief from their own average, lower, or lack of intelligence.

For Spiritualists, the surviving soul is uplifted to a higher level of intelligence. It is perhaps surmised that if an Infinite Intelligence exists forever, so too can individual intelligence ever exist. Those of lower intelligence who are unable to think for themselves are in need of a human-like intelligence or an intelligent god to think for them, and to furnish what is asked for. Therefore, it is assumed that the background of Infinite Intelligence serves as the causal mechanism to support survival of individual intelligence that upon dying continues to exist and does communicate with the living. Spiritualists seek the deceased and discarnate intelligence of family members, friends, and pets.

Taking conscious biological life to be a guideline, the soul, not the spirit or the breath, maintains the same structure developed on earth. The essence of the soul is a ninety to ninety-nine percent subconscious triune force of hunger for food, sex and reproduction, and aggression that forces the one to ten percent of the conscious self personality. It is the triune soul that compels each individual to continue.

Spiritualism advocates a one way progression of the soul through an afterlife existence. Spiritualists also advocate that the "doorway to reformation" is never closed, both here and hereafter. Reformation is defined as, "An improvement of personal behavior and thinking, to bring about beneficial change, to rescue from error or harm, and to return to a correct course."

Since no real higher and infinite intelligence exists to reform an individual, each has the onerous task of reforming thoughts and behaviors both on earth and in an afterlife. An individual soul is not instantly cured or reformed by an infinite intelligence, and the majority of Spiritualists do not have the intelligence to reform themselves. In reality, Spiritualists cannot depend on a pantheistic quasi order and disorder of cause and effect they label, Infinite Intelligence.

Spiritualism

For some years I lived in a small Spiritualist community, and while there I observed the following. The religion of Spiritualism attracts a variety of visitors; the curious, some grieving, and some seeking answers to and solace from life's turmoil. Some seek information about their own psychic or mediumistic experiences of dreams, ghosts and hauntings.

Of those who visit Spiritualist communities, some few may seek to become a member of the religion. Of those who do become members, most are eccentric misfits, and most lack education or are under educated. Spiritualist communities attract members looking for meaning and acceptance in life when they really should be consulting a psychotherapist. I personally observed that the religion of Spiritualism attracts members who exhibit psychological disorders ranging from neurosis to sociopath. Most members would be unable to successfully pass the MMPI (Minnesota Multiphasic Personality Inventory) test successfully. The question-response test consists of six scales that measure various areas of psychopathology.

Most good mediums are born with an ability obtained from family genetics or past lives. Study and practice can only polish the heritable talent. The Spiritualism education program does include student experiential practice of giving messages and mini-readings to the public. The academic, which is a misnomer, education program of the particular community I resided in is laughable, pitiful, and sad. At one low point, the test given at the end of required study to measure comprehension of the religion, consisted of ten brief questions.

One individual who completed the course of study and requested to take the final qualifying test, was so poor in reading and writing skills that he requested to take the ten question quiz orally.

The religion of Spiritualism is a miserable failure in ethics and fails to develop a method or practice of reducing the ego. Spiritualism even increases the sense of ego by accepting the view they will survive to continue on in an afterlife.

Few members who claim to be mediums actually have an authentic ability for communication with an afterlife dimension. Some practice by faking it hoping the ability will become real at some time in the future. There are a few authentic Spiritualist mediums who do an admirable job of providing convincing evidence for continued existence in an afterlife. Yet most Spiritualist mediums are of doubtful ability, mediocre, and some are outright frauds.

Members of the Spiritualist religion who have no talent for mediumship, turn to politics in the community, and cause much dissension and havoc. They compete for political control causing an undercurrent of negative opposition. The only ethic emphasized in Spiritualism is the trite platitude of the Golden Rule. This leaves room for an abundance of gossip, bickering, and backbiting, while hypocrisy is rampant. I eventually came to conclude that the particular community that I resided in, was not a religion but is either a political association or a business and financial association that conducts religious rituals.

Irrespective of its small membership numbers, and high percentage of deluded and dysfunctional members, the great message of Spiritualism is that humans are not dependent on a human-like god. It is the soul that is most important and real. The unique focus of Spiritualism is about being in the presence of souls and an afterlife, not a human-like god.

Though small, the practice of Spiritualism is a religion that will continue into the future. This is so even though it is regarded by most of science as superstition, by some religions as evil, and by skeptics as fraudulent.

In Spiritualism no god or devil can assist or resist humans but departed souls can assist and inspire and guide. Dimensional reality has been shown to exist through testing of mediums conducted by the Society for Psychical Research founded in 1882 in London with the stated purpose to "examine allegedly paranormal phenomena in a scientific and unbiased way."

The American Society for Psychical Research founded in 1884 has tested and continues to investigate many mediums today. The Parapsychological Association was formed in the United States in 1957 for the stated purpose "to advance parapsychology as a science, to disseminate knowledge of the field, and to integrate the findings with those of other branches of science." The Association continues to scientifically test and publish results in journal format in the main areas of psi including clairvoyance, telepathy, precognition, remote viewing, and medium-ship.

Life Challenge

Life is a challenge to comprehend both physical and metaphysical reality. Most humans fail to even adequately comprehend physical reality of the environment and the biology of life. For the great majority, metaphysical comprehension consists of only the traditional superficial belief of a human-like god. Developing better physical and metaphysical comprehension contributes to personal security both on earth and any possibility of a reality dimension that awaits thereafter.

Physical skills include comprehension of the body and brain functions, the development and maintaining of mental and physical health through proper diet and exercise, much education and learning, work skills and earning a living, and getting along with family, friends, and fellow humans.

Metaphysical skills include the cultivation of a consistent meditation discipline that contributes to development of extrasensory perception abilities.

The most important metaphysical skill is to develop the comprehension that a human-like god is an imaginary companion and a human artistic depiction, and that the soul is a real triune force of hunger for food, sex and reproduction, and aggression that forces life to life and survive.

Nothing or oblivion is unimaginable, there must be some substratum that always exists. Yet eternity has no eye with which to see, or no I with which to know. The always existing on its own is not a human-like god but is a sole cosmological force, field, or ground. The science of physics has empirically verified the second law of thermodynamics, known as, the law of conservation of energy. It categorically states, "the total energy of a closed system cannot be created or destroyed but changes and is conserved over time." It must then be acknowledged that the energy and force of the triune soul of the human body, is a continuation of a sole cosmological force, and is only relatively destructible and therefore is conserved through time change and dimensions.

Both the busyness of living and laziness distract from an approach to comprehension of life to be a continuation of a metaphysical cosmological force. Each is stretched thin by the multitude of duties in daily life that distract and so ignore this sublime truth and instead accept a shallow social belief of a human-like god. Yet if fortunate, for a few may come from time to time a beatific experience and vision, a numinous beatitude of being a continuation of the earth and a cosmological force that forever exists on its own.

Best

The earth while good is also bad or evil as fluctuating conditions bring about earthquakes, volcanos, drought and desert conditions, and violent storms and floods. While many life forms are beneficial and good for food and many make good pets, many more are harmful such as large predators, poisonous snakes, disease-spreading locusts, flies, and mosquitos, and microorganisms such as particular viruses, bacteria, and parasites. A minority of humans are ethical and good, while a majority are aggressive and violent, lie, and steal.

Since there is sufficient convincing evidence that the environment, life forms, and humans are both good and evil, they are clearly not the best.

Everyone likes what is best in life and will attempt to obtain what is best for personal comfort, especially money, desired possessions, and relationships. This situation begs a question. What is the best? Generally, what is best is what is helpful and can improve human life.

Though surrounded and supported by others, an individual must face life alone, and all too frequently encounters disappointment, betrayal, and verbal and physical harm by fellow humans. Even those who are closest will from moment to moment, or eventually betray another by disagreeing, and by willfully differing and going another way in life. This is the existential tension of making life choices.

What exceeds human ability and limitations can better manage life, and is thought to be the best. To be allied with the best that existence has to offer is sought. For many the best that existence has to offer is to know the beginning of it, and this where a human-like god is inserted to identify it. For many what is imagined to be most helpful in the struggle of life is a human-like genealogical first father god.

What is best for theists is the origin of the environment and life. The beginning of existence is imagined and artistically fashioned with words to be a human-like first father god. Theists then consider themselves to be connected to the best, and each considers himself to be the best he can be. Paired up with an imagined human-like first father god, an individual considers himself to be the best.

For many the best in life is prized to be a human-like god. A human father begets children while the metaphor of a biblical first father god begets the environment, life, and issues commands from his thoughts and mouth. The human father is real but the first father god is an unreal metaphor. For a great many, the metaphor supported only by blind faith, is prized as a certain and undoubted true identification of the origin of the environment and life.

In reality, it is best to correctly see that a human-like god is an adult version and continuation of a childhood imaginary companion, and that all theistic scriptures are an artistic word portrait made by humans. The best is to correctly comprehend the soul to be a triune force of hunger for food, sex and reproduction, and aggression that forces life to live. The best is to see that the soul has not been fashioned by a human-like god but is a continuation of the earth that is in turn a continuation of a cosmological force that moves the multiverse.

While living, what is best in life is to comprehend it. The personal accomplishment to be most proud of in life, is to become an astute observer of body, brain, and environment. When sensations are observed to be fleeting, and picture images come to a rest in now moments, then arises the thrill of freedom and health. However, this is relative as life is seen for what it really is, a continuing low rolling boil of hunger for food, sex and reproduction, and aggression, always ready to act to live and survive by now eating, now sex and reproduction, and now aggression. Once clearly observed, the boil of life must be meditatively monitored daily, moderated, and directed to pragmatic and beneficial results. True salvation is to reduce the soul, not to hold on to it or to save it.

While life seldom works out for the best, the best way to live is to achieve moderate success in the following areas of endeavor.

Health
Education/knowledge
Work/finances
Relationships

Most seek to have and enjoy the best in life but many only manage to obtain the worst. For those who fail in the competitive contest, the best of life is the relief of when it is over. Yet even this ending is just a beginning, whether of oblivion or an afterlife.

www.ingramcontent.com/pod-product-compliance
Lightning Source LLC
Chambersburg PA
CBHW071057280326
41928CB00050B/2537